SOLO TRAVEL IN A RELATIONSHIP

Break Through Barriers to Your Solo Journey

JENNY MOWBRAY

Solo Travel in a Relationship:
Break Through Barriers to Your Solo Journey
Jenny Mowbray

Published by Orchids to Olives

ISBN: 978-1-3999-2632-4

Cover Design by nskvsky
Formatting and Layout by Nonon Tech & Design

TABLE OF CONTENTS

INTRODUCTION

What is this book about?

This book is about travelling solo, or the desire to travel solo, when you are in a relationship.

Why does this require a book? Surely, if you want to go on a solo holiday then you just tell your partner and off you go.

Maybe, but it's not always that simple.

Over the last decade, there has been a huge increase in the number of women travelling solo, and why not? It is a fantastic way to travel – it's empowering, you get to see the world on your own terms and it's a great way to meet new people. In a nutshell, it's awesome. However, the general perception persists that solo travel belongs to the world of the singletons and although this view is slowly starting to shift, many women in relationships encounter a variety of barriers when they begin contemplating their own solo journey.

Honestly ladies, I think it's time to banish this outdated notion for good. It doesn't seem very fair to me. Why should single women get to pop on their travelling flip flops and set off into the world alone, whilst us loved up women put our solo flip flops aside?

Let's begin by banishing some common myths right now:

Myth 1 – solo travel is just for young single people.

Absolutely not – whatever your age, your relationship status or your travel experience – the solo travel door is yours to open.

Myth 2 – solo travel is a sign your relationship is in trouble.

No no no! The desire to travel solo when you are in a relationship is NOT a sign that your relationship is about to head to the dogs. On the contrary, it's a sign that you want to do something that excites you and your soul aches to explore alone.

Myth 3 – your relationship will suffer if you travel solo.

Let's banish that myth right now. When you travel solo your relationship WILL NOT suffer. There are a multitude of personal and relationship benefits. It may strengthen, revitalise and even bring new passion to your relationship.

Of course, this is not a 100% guarantee. There are no guarantees in life. I'm not claiming that solo travel can mend a rocky relationship or indeed skyrocket your sex life, but if you and your partner are committed to being together, solo travel is not something to fear it's something to embrace. It's symbolic of your love and commitment.

I want to travel solo, but...

It's easy for us to talk about the benefits of solo travel, but the reality of taking that first step towards your solo adventure is not always quite so easy.

Many women in relationships come up against challenges when considering a solo trip. Challenges that stop them from venturing forth and challenges that can sometimes shake tightly woven beliefs about what a relationship is and how people in a relationship should act.

This book will explore some of these challenges including:

- Does wanting to travel solo make me selfish?
- How do I broach the subject of solo travel with my partner?
- How can I reduce my partner's fears?
- Could I cope in the world alone?

Who is this book for?

This book is for you if:

- You're in a relationship and you have a burning desire to travel solo.
- You're curious about the benefits of travelling solo in a relationship.
- You think your partner will freak out if you mention solo travel.
- Your partner is freaking out because you mentioned solo travel.
- You want to travel solo, but you're scared.
- You're a single solo traveller who's contemplating entering a relationship and you're worried that it will mean the end to your solo adventures.
- You're the partner of someone who wants to travel solo, and you just don't get it.

Who am I?

As I slowly breathe in the rich tang of heady citrus blossoms in a Sorrento lemon garden, tears glisten in relief. I savour every single delicious moment from waking up in my charming single bedroom to gazing out at the radiant turquoise ocean, as the sun sets over the magnificent Vesuvius. Why did I wait so long? (Diary entry, 2009)

I was 37 when I took my first proper solo holiday to Italy and wrote that diary entry. In the warmth of the Italian spring, I gained my first real glimmer and a gentle prod of realisation that in order for me to grow, blossom and truly be myself I needed to follow a passion that had ached in my heart for as long as I could remember. I needed to venture out into the world alone.

It was the first of many solo trips and in the following ten years I would take many more, at first in Europe and then to Southeast Asia and Indonesia. I had been well and truly bitten by the solo travel bug, and I was smitten, so much so that I developed a flexible freelance career so I could travel more often.

However, a funny thing happened when I met a man and fell in love. People around me including friends and family presumed that my desire to travel solo would change, as if it would somehow evaporate overnight in a puff of smoke simply because I was in a relationship. Furthermore, when it became clear that I planned to continue my solo adventures, there was this strange notion that my partner wouldn't like it or support it. I was asked questions about whether he would trust me, whether he would worry about me, would he be able to cope alone and most alarming whether I thought our relationship would survive.

I became very curious.

This book stems from that curiosity.

Who I am not

Before you read this book, I think it's important for me to begin by telling you who I am not.

I'm not a relationship expert, far from it! I am writing this book because I have a passion for solo travel, and I don't want people in relationships to miss out. It's really that simple.

Any advice given in this book is a result of personal experience, personal reflection, research and conversations with friends and other solo travellers. The advice and tips are offered for you to ponder. Take from the book what works for you and disregard anything that doesn't resonate.

Relationships by their very nature are diverse and complex, so it would be impossible to cover the intricacies of all scenarios. Therefore, the advice is meant as a starting point. The rest is up to you.

My hope is that when you finish reading, you and your partner will feel much more comfortable with the idea of solo travel, and you will be ready to embark on your first solo adventure.

Please note:
Throughout this book I shall refer to you the reader as a woman and your partner as a man. This is because I am using my own experience, and these are my reference points.

HOW IS THIS BOOK STRUCTURED?

The book is divided into four main parts:

Part 1 – The Benefits of Solo Travel

We will begin by delving into the myriad of benefits that solo travel can bring to you on both a personal and relationship level. We'll discover why solo travel can be deeply enriching for your relationship.

Part 2 – Potential Challenges

We'll then come head on with why solo travel is often regarded as a big no when you're in a relationship and how we can firmly once and for all knock that outdated rusty peg from the wall.

We'll dive in and explore common challenges and look at some strategies for overcoming them.

Journaling/discussion prompts – throughout this section I have provided prompts that you may find helpful. There are some that could be used for personal reflection and a way of gathering your thoughts, and others that you may find helpful to use as discussion points with your partner.

Activities – I've also included some suggestions of activities you may like to try, both alone and with your partner.

Part 3 – Stories from 6 Women in Relationships Who Travel Solo

Travelling solo is great, but don't just take my word for it! Be inspired by the stories of six other women. They come from all walks of life and live across the globe, but what brings them together is their love of adventure and stepping out into the world alone.

Part 4 – Get Practical

The last section contains some tips for maintaining a strong bond whilst you're away, practical advice for going solo, useful apps and a few ideas on how to practice being more mindful.

PART 1

THE BENEFITS OF SOLO TRAVEL

Part 1

THE BENEFITS OF SOLO TRAVEL

If you haven't yet experienced travelling solo, you may be wondering what all the fuss is about. Why are so many women setting off on solo adventures? What's with this sudden urge to leave friends and loved ones behind? Surely, it's more fun to travel with someone isn't it? It may indeed seem perplexing and yet if you're curious...if a whisper from inside is gently urging you to discover your own solo journey, there is probably a valid reason for it, and I'd gently urge you to listen to that whisper.

Travelling with friends and family is great. I don't think there are many women who would claim to just want to travel solo and eliminate loved ones from the equation. I expect this would make for some very tricky conversations. I love all types of travel equally - a beach holiday in Greece with my partner – yes please! Sampling street food in Penang with my grown-up son - yes please! A girlie trip to Istanbul – Yes! A solo yoga retreat in Bali – oh yes, bring it on!

Where's the rule that says we should choose one over the other?

Travelling solo offers a very different experience. It's rarely simply a holiday. It gives you the unbridled freedom to experience the world on your own terms. It's uniquely personal and can be deeply enriching.

The next two chapters are dedicated to exploring the wealth of benefits associated with solo travel. Firstly, we'll look at the personal benefits and then we'll delve into the wealth of benefits for your relationship.

Of course, it would be a mistake to see the two sets of benefits as entirely separate entities because they're not at all. When your life is entwined within a relationship, each partner's happiness is fundamental to the wellbeing of the relationship as a whole. However, for the purpose of clarity, in the next few pages we are going to focus solely on you! Yes - you you you - and why solo travel might just be one of the best things you'll ever do.

Chapter 1

THE PERSONAL BENEFITS OF SOLO TRAVEL

Travel Deeper and Travel Your Way

I wondered why it was that places are so much lovelier when one is alone.

– Daphne Du Maurier

Discovering a new destination on your own is very different to experiencing it with someone else; not necessarily better, but definitely different. Alone, you are acutely more aware of your surroundings. It's as though your senses sharpen, and the world becomes richer in texture, smell, taste and sound – your eyes zoom in on the finer details, colours seem more vivid, people more animated, tastes more satisfying, smells more intense and sounds more invigorating.

Imagine for a second holding your favourite sweet-smelling flower and breathing in its delectable aroma. In that moment, your whole being is focused on that enchanting smell. Everything else drops away, it's just you and the flower. Well, that's a little like solo travel - a full invigorating sensory immersion, that leaves you wanting more.

Solo travel enables you to push all unwanted distractions aside, so that you can appreciate the full throng of a location in all its glory. It also enables you to travel your way and at your own pace, which is immensely satisfying.

A personal example: Sri Lanka – itinerary vs. my way

The first time I visited Sri Lanka was with a dear friend for my 40th birthday. Gorgeous hotels were booked – everything from beachside boutique to classy rainforest hideaways. An itinerary was planned with beach time, safaris, gem mines and tea factories. We 'did' the famous cultural triangle and put big ticks in the bucket list boxes including the awe inspiring Sigiriya Lion Rock and the amazing cave temples of Dambulla.

It was everything I could've wanted for my 40th birthday. And yet, something was missing. I felt empty. I felt like a voyeur. I felt out of touch with myself and my surroundings.

To be honest, I felt like a spoilt brat because there I was on a holiday of a lifetime, and I felt empty. I knew it wasn't the place. I fell in love with Sri Lanka on that trip and have returned three times since. So, what was it?

My answer came on a day when I spent some time alone. I was starting to feel a bit tetchy and so it made sense for my friend and I to spend some time apart. I decided to visit the historical Buddhist temple, The Temple of the Tooth, in Kandy by myself. It was on the itinerary after all.

I draped a light shawl over my shoulders, removed my shoes and with a flower offering of sweet jasmine silently made my way through the temple. The outside world, the itineraries and the hotels dropped away. Quietly, I lay my flowers at the altar of the central temple, sat down with my back against the cool wall and took in the surroundings – the heady floral incense, the gentle chanting of monks, the colourful mounds of purple and white flowers and the ancient ornate architecture. I felt my whole being breathe a big sigh of relief and relax. My emotions levelled and I began to feel like 'me' again.

As I left the temple buildings, with no awareness of the time, I strolled barefoot through the gardens, feeling the warmth of the paving radiating through my feet and a grounded sense of peace. I knew then with absolute certainty that I needed to return to Sri Lanka. Alone.

Eight months later, I stepped off the flight into the tropical heat on my first solo trip to Sri Lanka. This time I would spend part of my trip volunteering and the rest exploring the country my way. I didn't have a schedule of things I wanted to see and only a rough idea of where I wanted to go. I took my time. I meandered through chaotic colourful markets, bought fruit I'd never heard of, took long jostling train journeys and marvelled at the magnificent verdant landscape as I listened to the Sinhalese and Tamil dialect bursting through my European ears. I watched wild giant turtles surfing the waves, listened to the gentle creaks of bamboo swaying in the sultry breeze and was satiated by delicious mouthfuls of rice and curry bursting with aromatic spices. And this time when I padded barefoot through the Temple of the Tooth with my pretty flower offering, I did so because my heart guided me to, not because it was a 'must see' on my itinerary.

I travelled through the country the way I wanted to, and my heart was full to bursting.

You see, my preferred way of travelling was not the same as my friend's. I'm not a planner, I do not like itineraries – they stress me out. I like to feel my way and take in the subtleties of a location. I travel to experience, to feel and to learn about myself and the people around me. That doesn't mean I don't want to visit historic sites or art galleries, on the contrary, but it does mean that I don't like planning a trip around those sites with a tight time schedule.

We're all different, and whether you're a planner or a fly by the seat of your pants type woman, the beauty of solo travel is that you get to travel your way. You can do exactly what you want, and nobody will question you. What's more you can change your mind at the drop of a hat and not annoy anyone!

Such a relief.

Freedom!

She had not known the weight, until she felt the freedom.

– N. Hawthorne

What does freedom feel like to you?

For me, freedom, is that expansive feeling, of wanting to open your arms wide, breathe deep and laugh out loud to the world; where the weight of responsibility drops away and an open vista of possibility reaches out in all directions. Solo travel gives you that fabulous feeling in bucket loads.

There is nothing quite like that feeling of checking in your luggage at the airport, knowing that in several hours' time your passport will be stamped and out you'll step into a whole new environment ready to be explored.

As a solo traveller, you have the added exciting anticipation of not only going on holiday, but also having the complete freedom to choose what you want to do and when you'll do it.

Freedom from Looking for Mr Right

Are you a woman who travelled solo when you were single?

If the answer is yes, you may wonder whether you'll feel that same sense of freedom now that you're in a relationship. I'm happy to report, from my own personal experience, that yes, I certainly do. And what may surprise you, is that I feel an even greater sense of freedom. That may sound like a contradiction, why would I feel freer? Well, it's simple, unlike my former single self I was no longer on the lookout for Mr Right.

Yes, yes I know, I know shoot me down! As a single independent woman of the world, I shouldn't have been eyeing up every wandering Romeo! But let's face it, when you're single, you're never too many steps away from wondering if the next man you meet might just be 'the one' or at the very least, the one up for a little romantic dalliance…ooh la la (my apologies to any the singletons who do not have a roaming eye such as mine. I am merely reflecting on my personal experience and my fondness for a light flirting).

Anyway, I digress, the point is knowing that you are in a stable committed relationship gives you the immense sense of emotional freedom to really embrace the experience of travel to its fullest.

There are no distractions, it's just you and the world.

Solo Travel and Personal Growth

We have a choice in life, to be open and be what we can be, or to be closed and be less than we are.

– Paul Linden

Solo travel is fantastic for personal growth.

Personal growth is one of those ubiquitous buzz expressions, but what does it mean and why is it important?

It means branching out of your comfort zone so that you can grow as a person and live a life that is deeply enriching and fulfilling. It's about letting your roots dig down and allowing the branches of possibility to shoot out and bud.

Personal growth is about NOT standing still, NOT becoming stale and NOT thinking you're the finished product at whatever age you currently are. It's knowing that you are a constant work in progress (if you allow yourself to be) until the day you leave this planet.

We all have a comfort zone. It's that place that feels safe, a place where you can predict what will happen. That place might be cosy, but does it truly allow you to be all that you can be?

Stepping out of your comfort zone into your unknown takes bravery, but when you do magical things start to happen. Magic? Yes magic. Right now, you don't know how you might grow. That's the thing about the unknown, you can't predict it – it's impossible. You can't predict the experiences you may have, the people you may meet, nor the opportunities that may come your way. However, one thing that is certain, once you step over that invisible barrier of comfort you are destined to grow in one way or another.

Does personal growth require solo travel? No, of course not. You can step out of your comfort zone in many ways – learn to tango, skydive, sail – but I'm presuming that because you are reading this book you have a passion for travel, and the urge to travel solo is nibbling away at your psyche in some way.

How will I grow?

Oh, the possibilities are endless my dear – you might get better at problem solving, your social skills may improve, you may even learn a new language or become an ace surfer; and whilst you're at it, you'll gain confidence and become much more comfortable with yourself.

There's certainly not enough room in this book to discuss all the potential growth opportunities. However, let's take a look at some of the common areas of personal growth:

Ms Self Reliant and Problem Solver Extraordinaire

Learning to navigate the world alone, however daunting this may seem at first, is a fantastic skill to have and a huge self-esteem booster.

Travelling solo, means that you need to get practical. There's no getting away from the fact that you've got to figure stuff out for yourself – everything from train timetables, airport transfers, money conversions, language challenges, where to get dinner and how to find your hotel.

When you travel with a companion, there's a natural tendency to share the responsibility of figuring stuff out. Maybe you're already someone who likes to take the lead or maybe you're the complete opposite, and you're happy to leave it to someone else. Often, it's not a conscious decision to divvy out roles, rather you'll simply work things out together and with that shared decision making there's a certain amount of reassurance.

Who are you - leader, passenger, partner?

Travelling solo requires you to make all those decisions yourself and by doing so, you not only acquire new skills, but you start to trust your own judgement and grow in confidence.

Fortunately, the internet has made life a whole lot easier than it was even ten years ago. There are not many places on the planet these days where you can't get access.

However, the internet can't do everything – sure you can check in for your flight online, book a train from Paris to Marseille, book a youth hostel in Vietnam, check how many rupees are to the pound and translate bread into Spanish, but you've still got to have plenty of real life good old savvy about you. Google is one thing but using Google maps to navigate the maze of roads in the heat of the summer in Rome when you keep losing the Wi-Fi signal is another matter entirely (speaking from very personal experience)!

Also, don't for one minute think that a solo trip needs to be some wild adventure to the back and beyond to enable you to benefit from picking up new travel skills. You don't need to go backpacking around Southeast Asia to reap the rewards. A solo beach holiday to Spain still requires travel savviness, especially if it's your first solo trip. Just think of all the things you need to do alone even on a regular beach holiday – airport shenanigans, public transport, finding the hotel, finding your way around, eating in restaurants alone (often a biggie for first timers), buying things in a language you don't speak...If you've never done any of these things alone before, they are a big deal, and you will learn new skills.

Fine Tune Your Social Butterfly Skills

There are no strangers here; only friends you haven't met yet.

– Yeats

One of the main questions solo travellers get asked is, 'don't you get lonely?' and most will tell you no. Travelling solo is a great way to meet fascinating people from all walks of life. Furthermore, it can enhance your communication and fine tune your social butterfly skills.

Why?

Travelling alone is very different to travelling with a companion. When you are with someone else, you already have a cosy friendship bubble, which is much less penetrable than the glowing aura of friendly openness presented by you the solo traveller. Alone you are naturally more open to meeting new people, both locals and fellow travellers; your body language is that of 'hey, let's chat' as opposed to 'hey, we're having so much fun together we don't really need anyone else.'

Locals are much more likely to offer their help when you're alone and take an interest in what you're doing. On solo trips, local women have stopped to talk to me in the street, café owners have sat down and told me their life stories and strangers have offered me home cooked food. This rarely happens when I'm with a companion.

There's also a camaraderie of mutual recognition that exists between solo travellers wherever you go in the world. You are away from the familiar in a fresh environment and you already have something pretty cool in common, so it's relatively easy to strike up a conversation. In fact, whether you already regard yourself as socially confident, or not, it's likely that you'll become very adept at starting conversations with strangers.

When you meet someone travelling, there is no previous history and, in all likeliness, you'll probably never see them again. Armed with this knowledge, a genuine space of authentic interaction can take place, which is very liberating.

Those annoying worries that our unruly minds are prone to concocting – you know the ones - whether you said something dumb, whether you inadvertently offended someone…are given the chance to melt away. You may of course, be much more chilled out than me, but I hold my hand up to sometimes being annoyingly self-conscious and allowing my thoughts to sabotage my confidence. Solo travel enables you to practice quietening that irritating inner voice to simply enjoy chatting to strangers in the present moment.

The enduring benefit of learning to interact with ease whilst travelling, is that it flows into your 'normal' everyday life, giving you the ability and confidence to converse with a wide range of people in your home life, from the workplace to social gatherings.

You Learn a Lot About Yourself

And the day came when the risk to remain tight in a bud was more painful than the risk it took to blossom.

– Anais Nin

Solo travel and self-discovery go hand in hand. As soon as you step out into the world alone, you step into the world of learning who you are.

This is a time to shed the many masks you may wear back home, whether this be wife, professional, parent, daughter and so on. We all wear masks to a certain degree as part of our daily life – I know I wear a different mask when I am interacting with work colleagues to when I am with a friend. Some masks are thicker than the others, some just a light translucent wash and others harder, less prone to cracks. Sometimes we don't even realise we're wearing a mask, until we leave our familiar environment; and with a sweeping sense of relief, our masks silently slip away, and you're left with you.

As you move through your journey solo, you will start to learn more about yourself, what you like, what you don't like, what sits well and what doesn't. We could talk about a whole array of things here, from discovering a love of sand boarding in the desert, the stark realisation that you hate museums and will never step foot in one again or the highly important acknowledgement that no matter where you are in the world you can't shake the need for morning coffee! Perhaps, you'll even learn that you hate solo travel and never want to do it again, well great – that's that figured out! One to tick off the list.

These are all important discoveries, but regardless of your individual likes and dislikes, it boils down to, peeling back the layers, shedding the metaphorical masks to discovering your true beautiful authentic self. It's here where you find a strong sense of 'me,' and this is where real inner strength emerges.

The True Value of Learning What Rocks Your Heart into Bliss

When you do things from your soul you feel
a river moving in you, a joy.

– Rumi

I use the words soul, spirit, heart, core, and authentic self a lot in this book. I use these words to refer to that part of you that you know without question is your true self, that internal place where you feel most content and happy. I use these words a lot and unapologetically because I believe that each and every one of us should be doing our darndest to live OUR best life. Not your parents' idea of your best life, and not what your husband or best friend thinks. Your best life is an inside job and only you know what that is.

Living your best life, comes from really knowing who you are.

Most of us go through life being pulled in all different directions and being persuaded and influenced by a whole host of external factors which do not necessarily bring about internal happiness. In contrast, as you begin to strip back the masks on your solo journey, you discover what really rocks your heart into bliss and soothes your soul, and if you're like the many other solo adventuresses out in the world you may feel a contented joy wash over you. This is not the temporary joy gained from external sources, such as buying a new pair of shoes, but a joy that comes from deep within.

The first time I went on a solo holiday it was to bella Sorrento in Italy. For the duration of that trip, I felt so blissfully 'me' that I knew I had made the right decision to travel solo. My heart was giving me a big high five in thanks and I was filled to bursting with joy. However, the biggest and most important realisation I had on that holiday was that I needed to bring more of that feeling into my life because it had been sorely missing.

Around the same time, I came across the writer Joseph Campbell and his words radically changed how I approached life. He said 'Follow your bliss. If you do follow your bliss, you put yourself on a kind of track that has been there all the while waiting for you, and the life you ought to be living is the one you are living' (1991). In other words, when you follow your heart's desire, you put yourself on a path to living a life that is deeply fulfilling.

The true value of doing things that are aligned with your soul and learning what rocks your heart into bliss is that you begin to recognise more of what you need to do to keep that feeling flourishing. You begin to really know when something feels right for you and conversely when something feels wrong.

You become more inwardly attuned.

These realisations were a real game changer for me. I knew that my bliss was solo travel and so I put it centre stage, rather than on the periphery. I moved towards quitting my stressful teaching job and built a location independent freelance career so that I could follow my bliss.

I'm not suggesting that solo travel will lead you to make drastic life changes, but what I am suggesting is that when you follow that dancing spirit of yours on a solo travel journey, doors may open, opportunities you never imagined may present themselves or you may simply find yourself intuitively making decisions and attracting a way of being that feels right.

To see this in action, pop over to the stories written by six women who love travelling alone, in Part 3. For example, take Katherine, who followed her passion for packing light and created the informative blog, The 5 Kilo Traveller; or read about Sue-Anne whose desire for safe and affordable accommodation for women over fifty led to the creation of the SisterStay homestay community; or MJ whose love of travel and tea led to the sumptuous creation of The Silk Tea Co.

When you learn and do what rocks your heart into bliss, you'll not look back. You'll just keep bringing more of it into your life.

Solo Travel and Presence

Life isn't as serious as the mind makes it out to be.

– Eckhart Tolle

The concept of being present or mindful has firmly taken root in recent years as an antidote to stress and anxiety. There has been a great deal of research into happiness, with many experts agreeing that a strong prediction as to how happy you are is the ability to stay in the present moment.

Being present or mindful simply means being aware of your thoughts, and feelings in the present moment.

World renowned spiritual teacher, Eckhart Tolle suggests that 'as soon as you honour the present moment, all unhappiness and struggle dissolve, and life begins to flow with joy and ease. When you act out of the present-moment awareness, whatever you do becomes imbued with a sense of quality, care and love' (2004, p.67).

Sounds good, doesn't it? However, as most of us spend our waking hours wandering from one thought to another, it's easier said than done.

Solo travel gives you the perfect opportunity to experience and practice presence.

Imagine this. You're in Florence, sat at a pavement café in a bustling side street just off the Piazza Del Duomo. The Cathedral's striking terracotta dome towers in magnificence. Boxes of vibrant magenta geraniums adorn the window ledges. The sun shines bright. A fruit-seller opposite sells mounds of large ripe fragrant peaches, spears of fresh asparagus and crates of perfectly formed globe artichokes. People gather and chat animatedly. And there you are with your perfect Italian coffee. Perfectly present observing the scene playing out in front of you.

Where else do you need to be?

Well, you could be on your mobile, planning your next move, texting, reporting all you see on social media. However, if you choose, you can simply take in the joy of the present moment.

We can of course do this anywhere; we do not need to travel solo to practice being mindful. However, there are a few things that make practicing presence when we're travelling slightly easier. Firstly, the break from routine and lack of responsibility, helps to pull you out of those habitual thought patterns. Secondly, by being in a new location, away from familiar cues, you are giving your mind a little spring clean and thirdly, without a companion to distract you, you have every opportunity to savour the present moment.

There's a fabulous book, called Alone Time and I recommend it to all would be solo travellers. It provides guidance on how we can master presence whilst travelling and how we can continue to fine tune the art wherever we go (see Appendix: Resources).

Transferable Skills

The benefits I have discussed above are not confined to your trip, they are transferable skills and qualities for life. How many employers these days want people who are flexible, confident, good communicators and can use their initiative? Well, tell me, is there a better way to build these skills than being let loose in the world?

The benefits I talk of in this chapter, are an amalgamation of my own experience and other women that I have spoken to, but your story will be your own. Don't let anyone tell you how it should or shouldn't be. These words are from my heart to yours. They offer a starting point, a spyglass in which to begin and shed some light on what solo travel may offer to you. The benefits you discover along the way may be like mine or they may not. However, as you progress on your journey, I think it's safe to say that you'll discover new things about yourself. And when we learn about ourselves, we grow. We grow in self-knowledge, self-awareness and with that comes confidence and self-assurance.

Chapter 2

THE BENEFITS OF SOLO TRAVEL FOR YOUR RELATIONSHIP

Being deeply loved by someone gives you strength, while loving someone deeply gives you courage.

– Lao Tzu

Whether you want to take a short solo city break to Paris, a pampering retreat to Thailand or are setting off for several months on a solo travel adventure around the world, your relationship cannot only be maintained but thrive, and benefit greatly from the time apart.

Contrary to popular belief, being in a relationship is not a reason to push solo travel to the back of the 'something I would do if I were single' cupboard, being in a relationship is an excellent reason to jet off alone and soak up some enriching me time whilst at the same time giving your relationship a powerful boost.

In this chapter we will explore why solo travel can be the perfect energiser, passion dynamo and all-round relationship enhancer.

A Happy Relationship is Made Up of Happy Individuals

Two halves = a cup of overflowing love and happiness. Ahem... wrong!!

Whilst it might be true that in the passion filled throes of early infatuation, your new love may fill your love cup to bursting and with it a delicious sense of wholeness and wonderous happiness, in the long run these feelings wane and there's only one person left to fill your happy cup and that's you. Your partner could be the most loving, kind, and considerate person in the world but if you're down in the dumps because you're not following your dreams, they are not going to 'make' you happy and ultimately you and your relationship will suffer.

The key word is individuals.

Relationships are generally made up of two individuals who choose to be together because they really like each other's company. However, they are not responsible for each other's happiness.

Your happiness is your responsibility and as we saw in the last chapter if solo travel is something you are passionate and excited about it can be a route to greater personal fulfilment. This benefits not just you, but everyone around you, including your partner because when you feel happy and energised, your vitality radiates outwards touching all those close to you.

I think we all know people who seem to radiate energy and life, they are a joy to be around, they are stimulating, and you want to spend more time in their company. In contrast, you probably also know individuals who suck the living daylights out of you with their negativity and woe is me attitude. I know who I prefer to be around! Do you?

In the words of Elizabeth Lesser, a writer I much admire, 'if we try to love or lead, or work or pray, from a dry well, then we will serve up a bitter cup to those around us and never really live the life we were given' (2004, p.49).

Happiness is your calling, it's an inside job and when you make that decision to be in charge of it, you and your partner reap the rewards.

Absence Really Does Make the Heart Grow Fonder

Absence sharpens love, presence strengthens it.

– T Fuller

It's a cliché but there is much truth in it. Absence really does make the heart grow fonder.

If I could bottle that feeling of when I am returning home from a solo trip and sell it, I would be a rich woman. Why? Because it fizzes with delicious magical soul dancing skin tingling excitement!

When I fly back from a solo trip, watching the clouds drift below and ticking off the hours, the only thing in my heart is the anticipation and joy of being in my lover's arms again. On these return journeys, my excitement parallels the feelings of when we first met, but with an added depth.

And then, of course, there are the first few hours and days that we are together again…bliss.

I was telling a friend about this feeling of coming home joy, and she sceptically enquired 'so does it end after those few first days? Is it like having a fling and then getting bored and wanting to move on?' I could understand why she was asking. After the distance and the build-up of emotions, I could see why she may construe it to be an anti-climax after the initial buzz. However, my answer was of course not. I love my partner and yes sure the initial excitement subsides after a few days and normality prevails, but the periods of absence, sharpen and intensify our love, which permeates our relationship and further strengthens it.

It's an exquisite thing to miss someone and return back to them.

Increased Curiosity

A successful marriage requires falling in love many times, always with the same person.

– Mignon McLaughlin

Curiosity gives that sparkle and pizazz to relationships and keeps it fresh.

In any new relationship there is a strong element of curiosity. You want to know all there is to know about that person – whether they like spinach, whether they recycle, what they think about the colour blue…everything about them is new, fresh, and exciting. Each piece of new information is like unravelling a giant multicoloured pass the parcel game.

However, over time, the curiosity may diminish. You may feel you know all there is to know about your loved one. Maybe you finish their sentences, perhaps you've heard the same story more than once, you know their political views, you know that you'll go out for a meal on Friday and have sex twice a week, three times if you're lucky… In other words, you've unwrapped the many colourful layers and you are holding in your hand the slightly less riveting pass the parcel prize from a discount store.

Okay, okay! I'm being mean and generalising wildly, but you get the point.

As relationships unfold, there is a slight tendency for things to become a little routine and predictable. In marked contrast, when you embark on a solo travel adventure suddenly all that predictability is given a good old shake up and routine flies out the window. Curiosity is given the room to grow again.

Perhaps you no longer feel like you know everything about your partner. Maybe your conversations are richer and more inspiring, as you both dip into the pool of the unknown. Maybe, new ideas take root leading the way for new opportunities. Who knows? It's not for me to say. However, what I do know is that by giving your relationship the gift of curiosity, you're giving it the space for love to be revitalised and to flourish.

Absence therefore not only makes the heart grow fonder in the short term it also creates the feeling of space in your heart and mind for a revived sense of curiosity and this is such a beautiful feeling.

Passion and Intimacy

Solo travel can do wonders for your sex life.

Absence not only makes your heart grow fonder it can also give your libido a boost.

Sex and intimacy are fundamental to having a fulfilling and happy relationship. Solo travel is a great way to stoke the embers of passion and embrace the role of lovers.

Here are some ways, your sex life may be enhanced by a little distance:

Horny overdrive – a little absence in the bedroom department may have you lusting after your partner as though he has morphed into Brad Pitt overnight (or female equivalent). Many couples report that during the initial stages of being separated, libidos flat line in the knowledge that it's going to be a while before they see their loved one again. However, once they're over the half-way hump and the end is in sight, humping (pardon the pun) takes the limelight. It's not uncommon for an insatiable lust to set in and the desire to feel your partner, drives you and him slightly crazy (in a good way).

For me this sexual fervency is a feeling akin to when you first start dating. Do you remember the days when you couldn't imagine not wanting to ravish your lover every moment of the day? That's the feeling. Pretty hot hey?

Finding innovative ways to share your passion – one of the pleasures of being separated from your partner is the freedom to express your desire and finding ways to satiate it. From long lingering phone calls to sexting your passion, these days we have a whole range of multimedia options available to us at our fingertips. Arranging a virtual meeting may take on a whole new meaning. Alternatively, perhaps you prefer old school and want to write letters to light up your partner's day.

Sharing your passion, in whichever manner works for both of you, will no doubt put a spring in your step.

Discovery and exploring – you may find that the distance enables you to communicate your desires, your sexual preferences, and fantasies easier than in person.

Sometimes physical distance allows an openness to unfold that may not have otherwise happened, or certainly may have taken longer. There is a natural tendency to want to share more when you miss someone a lot. It's a way of bringing that person closer to you, a way of closing the physical gap. Therefore, don't be surprised if you discover new enticing things about your loved one and maybe you'll finally pluck up the courage to tell him...

Increased overall intimacy – finding ways to be intimate whilst a partner is away, is one thing, but the enduring effect is that it can open doors to better and stronger communication about sex overall leading to an added level of depth and satisfaction to your love making. In other words, you get to put into practice all those delicious things you've discussed during your time apart.

Throughout the process of writing this book, I have discussed it with my partner Scott to ensure it resonated with him and to maintain a balanced perspective. When he read this section, he agreed with the points I've discussed; however, he looked at me and exclaimed 'it's not all about sex Jenny! What about the romance?' And he's right of course, solo travel may bring a new dimension to your sex life, but the ability to use a range of communication technologies is also a truly romantic way to share your heartfelt feelings towards each other, which brings me nicely onto communication.

Improved Relationship Communication

Communication is to a relationship what breath is to life.

– Virginia Satir

Spending time apart can enrich communication. Sharing your day, your thoughts and feelings becomes an important way to feel close, and for many couples it becomes natural to want to share love, care and gratitude through regular communication.

In our routine daily lives, it's all too easy to get into the habit of a peck on the cheek and an 'I love you' before work, without really considering the meaning behind those three little words. The converse is true with time apart, the depth of meaning is everything and even the most diehard un-romantics can turn into budding poets.

Communication, both the ability to listen attentively and talk with meaning, is fundamental to any relationship. We all know this, and yet a common complaint between well-established couples is that they feel their partner doesn't always listen to them. There can be a tendency to half listen, nodding and going through the motions of listening, whilst concurrently thinking about other things – work, what to make for tea or the measurements for a perfect martini. It's not due to a lack of love, nor something we necessarily do purposefully. However, routine and familiarity can lead to that all too comical 'ah ha, oh really…that's interesting... yes dear' phenomena (I've noticed my Scott is particularly adept at this).

Taking a break from your familiar routine means that you do not talk simply because your partner is there in front of you with ready and available ears, but instead it is likely that there will be eagerness to *really* talk and *really* listen to each other.

Imagine that – no more 'yes dears...' and instead 'ooooh really tell me all about that darling!'

Furthermore, arranging a time to chat, especially if you are in a different time zone, adds a new dimension to when you can communicate. Personally, as I wait for our arranged chat time, I'm full of anticipatory excitement. I sometimes even get happy tummy butterflies!

Communication is the foundation for a successful solo trip, and we will return to this throughout this book.

Independence

Solitude is independence.

– Herman Hesse

Independence is important for a relationship because it shows that you are with that person because you choose to be, not because you need or rely on them. Independence gives you the self-knowledge that you can get by perfectly well by yourself, but you choose to be with your gorgeous partner because you love him to bits.

Some relationships struggle when one or both partners become too dependent on each other. Whilst it is of course great to support each other practically and emotionally, it's also important that you do this as individuals and because you want to, not because you feel compelled to. When you blindly expect that your partner always cooks dinner, is always there as your emotional sounding board, always navigates when you go on a trip…it can lead to resentment, or simply become tedious and boring.

Solo travel inevitability puts you in a situation where you have to be independent, nobody else is going to find the hotel and nobody else is going to make sure you're on the correct train. Furthermore, it places your partner in a situation where they must be independent, whether they are home, or they've decided to go off on their own adventure.

Independence feels good.

Trust

Loving someone is giving them the power to break your heart, but trusting them not to.

– Julianne Moore

What is a relationship without trust?

One of the most important aspects of any relationship is trust. Trust is the foundation from which a strong connection is formed. Without trust it's hard for a relationship to move beyond first base, thrive and progress to deeper levels.

Some may claim that solo travel is a test of trust; however, I would argue that if your relationship is already trust driven solo travel further reinforces that level of trust. In fact, in its most positive sense solo travel deepens trust and security between a couple, and further strengthens the relationship.

It's a great feeling to know that you can be apart for a prolonged period and that you trust each other implicitly.

We are all at different stages with trust, depending on previous experiences. If trust comes up as an issue, solo travel can be a way to bring those issues to the forefront and a way smooth over some of those rocky edges. We'll explore this in more detail in chapter 7.

Introverted Partners – a Time to Refresh

Solitude matters, and for some people, it's the air they breathe.

– Susan Cain

Solo travel offers introverted partners the perfect opportunity to refresh and revitalise.

In very simple terms, people who consider themselves introverts gain their energy from spending time alone and extroverts gain their energy from being around other people. Our brains are wired differently and what makes an extrovert buzz with excitement, can make an introvert feel overwhelmed and tired. It's an unfortunate fact that much of western society is geared up to the extrovert ideal from schooling to the workplace, to societal expectations of what you do on a Friday night. If you are interested in reading more about introverts, I wholeheartedly recommend Susan Cain's book *Quiet* or her TED Talks.

Speaking as an introvert myself, I need periods of solitude. Time alone is fundamental to my happiness and it's one of the reasons I love to travel solo.

Many introverts find that an extended period of alone time is akin to taking a very deep breath of air and letting it out very slowly in complete relief. This is not a relief to be away from loved ones, but the pure unadulterated relief of time alone. Time to just simply be.

Travelling solo offers abundant solitude from the very minute you set foot on your adventure.

I was trawling a Facebook group recently and somebody asked the question 'is it okay to just stay in your apartment and read when you're on a city break?' The woman commented that she felt a sense of guilt. My initial internal reaction was one of wow you're really asking this question. However, as I pondered, I realised that this question is actually a reflection of living in a society that extols the virtues of extroversion. In other words, to enjoy your time – you should be doing doing doing and if you're not then you feel guilty.

Whereas actually this woman's soul was saying to her I want to luxuriate in my beautiful apartment (that I've paid all this money for), feel the warmth of the sun as I read on my balcony, order a glass of wine from room service, bask in the glory of my own company, breathe and relax, whilst a life foreign to my own plays out below.

Solo travel is about doing exactly as you please, it's about tuning into yourself and not feeling like you should be doing something because that's what everyone else does, and that's what the guidebook says you should not miss. It's your holiday.

For all the introverts out there, who need their alone time, solo travel revitalises your heart, mind and soul. After experiencing this glorious unadulterated alone time, you will return to your partner feeling refreshed and energised. Ready to give and receive bountiful love.

Alone time is Good for Everyone

Alone time is when I distance myself from the voices of the world so I can hear my own.

– Oprah Winfrey

The merits of spending time alone are not just restricted to the partner who travels, but to both and whether your partner decides to stay at home or go on their own trip, they will also reap the rewards of some solo time. Research shows that spending time alone is healthy regardless of whether you are an introvert or extrovert.

Here are some of the benefits of solitude:

Improved concentration and memory – when you spend time alone, your attention becomes much more focused, which in turn improves memory (Carter, 2012).

Increased productivity – do you have something you really want to do but you keep putting it off? Time spent alone is perfect for finally getting that job done!

Enhanced creativity– throughout the centuries, artists, philosophers, innovators and writers have spoken of the need to spend time alone. Solitude is associated with enhanced creativity and concentration. Talented people from Shakespeare to Aldous Huxley, Monet to Lana Del Ray, Darwin to Steve Wozniak and Audrey Hepburn to Chrissie Hinde have spoken about the need for solitude (Rosenbloom, 2019).

Getting to know yourself – as discussed in chapter one, alone time is good for self-development. Time alone, gives you the opportunity to experiment and make your own choices without the influence of someone else's opinions. It allows us to gently reconnect with our inner selves, to reflect and find balance. This strengthens the relationship with ourselves, and in turn enables us to connect with others in a much healthier way.

Relaxation and reflection – in our hectic noise filled world, a chance for quiet can be a blessing. Spending time by ourselves, can be a time when we truly relax. If you've not experienced this for a while, it can be quite an eye opener and a window into the soul.

Different Holiday Preferences

There is a strange notion that when you are in a relationship you should automatically have the same holiday preferences, but for many couples this is simply not the case.

Travelling solo enables you both to go on the type of vacation you prefer. If you want to go trekking in the Andes but your partner prefers the art galleries of Paris, it's a no brainer that you go on these holidays separately. It makes sense not only on a personal interest level, but also financially – why waste the money going on a holiday that doesn't particularly appeal to both of you, when you can save that money by having independent holidays, followed by a joint holiday that you both really fancy?

Different Work Patterns

The pandemic has changed how we work. With hybrid or fully remote models of work becoming the new normal, many of us have been granted greater flexibility with regards to when and how we take vacations.

The impact, of course, varies depending on the type of job you do. If both partners have jobs that require them to attend their place of work, there is little change. However, for those couples who are now experiencing either one or both partners working from home, the freedom to spend part of this time in a different country has been opened up, meaning that for the first time many couples have greater scope to test the waters with solo travel.

Whilst writing this book I spent a portion of my time in the Canary Islands and in Sri Lanka. I guess you could call it a writing-cation. I have this flexibility because I work freelance, and I am not dependent on my location. In contrast, my partner is a college lecturer and doesn't have the same degree of flexibility.

So, I make the most of this situation and embrace my love of solo travel whilst continuing to work.

Blended Families

Families these days come in all shapes and sizes, and blended has become very much the norm with each or both partners bringing their own tribe to the mix.

The varying ages of children may provide the perfect opportunity for a spot of solo travel. This could ring true, particularly if one partner has grown up children whilst the other has little cherubs. Solo travel may be the perfect answer for some much-needed self-care time.

In this chapter we have explored some of the benefits of solo travel for your relationship. The most important message is that solo travel can be a gift to your relationship. It can deepen your connection to each other, whilst bringing about greater personal and relationship happiness.

PART 2

POTENTIAL CHALLENGES

Part 2

POTENTIAL CHALLENGES

The next section deals with common challenges that arise when thinking about taking a solo holiday when you are in a relationship. Let's face it, there is a reason you are reading this book. What is it? What's the challenge?

Are you thinking about solo travel but feeling unsure about taking the leap into the world alone without your partner? Or perhaps, you know without a doubt that this is something you really want to do but your partner is not so enthralled by the idea?

Wherever you are in that decision making process, this chapter will deal with some common challenges that many women in relationships face when contemplating solo travel.

The purpose of the next few pages is to delve into these challenges, shine some light on them and discuss strategies to overcome them and hopefully reduce worries.

The potential challenges covered in the next few chapters cannot account for every couples' individual circumstance, this would be impossible, and every relationship is different, with its own set of dynamics and challenges. However, based on chatting with friends, conducting surveys, quizzing my own partner and of course using my personal experiences the issues discussed are common themes.

Chapter 3

I MUST BE SO SELFISH!

What resonates with your deepest self is usually what is best for all those around you, even if they don't like it at the time.

– Regina Thomashauer

Is this a familiar thought?

'Look at me wanting to travel solo to far flung countries without my other half! What's wrong with me? I'm so selfish!'

If you can relate to this, you're not alone, many women in relationships contemplating their first solo holiday have very similar thoughts.

However, let me ask you some very important questions:

Is it selfish to pursue things that bring you joy?

Is it selfish to pursue things that empower you?

Is it selfish to pursue things that give you confidence?

Is it selfish to want the bring the best of yourself to all of your relationships?

In the previous chapters, we discussed the importance of doing things that bring you joy. When your personal wellbeing is enhanced, it reverberates and adds a powerful zing to all your relationships including your partnership or marriage. Your happiness is good for everyone else around you, including your loved ones.

Inner happiness creates more of the good stuff. It's addictive! And it's your job to create it, no one else can do it for you.

But I have a great partner…I should be happy!

Do you negate your feelings and rationalise that you don't really need to do this solo travel thing? Perhaps your internal dialogue goes along the lines of 'wow I really am so lucky, I have this amazing partner, great friends, lovely house, I have...I have… (fill in the blanks) so I should be really happy!'

Tricky right?

No not really, if there's something inside you that's calling to your soul there will always be something missing. Like an itch you just can't scratch. A dull ache that needs to be set free and I'm afraid to say that try as they may, your partner, your friends, or your family can't scratch that itch for you. Only you can.

It's your responsibility.

It's not selfish to want to follow your heart.

What Do YOU Want?

When you push down your own desires and moderate your behaviour in order to avoid possible conflict, it invariably brings about a great deal of personal unhappiness and can eventually sour the happiest of relationships.

Whilst both men and women may do this to a degree, studies have shown that women are far more likely to feel the need to negate their own desires to please their partner than the other way around. It's therefore crucial to be aware of the role that our gender plays in how we interact with our loved ones.

Gender studies have repeatedly shown that traditionally girls are raised to be pleasant, to care for others, not to speak up for what they want and to please people. The expectation that a woman will put others' needs before her own is deeply ingrained into our society and continuously reinforced. As Regina Thomashauer comments 'you are trained to ignore your happiness and pay attention to other cues' (2014, p.18). The same cannot be said for men.

Consequently, as women we are more likely than men to dampen down our own desires in a bid to make others feel happy and when it comes to intimate relationships, women are more likely to repeatedly ask 'what do you want?' 'What can I do to make you feel happy?' and then adapt and moderate their own behaviour to fit. This is fine to a degree, being caring is part and parcel of being in a relationship. However, the damage occurs when one half of the couple perpetually puts the needs of the other first, at the expense of their own emotional needs. It ultimately, leads to resentment and unfulfillment.

I am of course simplifying a complex subject and our perception of gender is evolving. Today, conscientious parents are adopting parenting techniques that don't reinforce gender stereotypes. And now we women are considerably more aware of the impact that upbringing, cultural and societal expectations have on our behaviour. However, we cannot ignore the impact that gender socialisation has on our behaviour, the behaviour of others towards us and how it influences our interactions with our partners.

It's therefore important to turn the viewfinder inward and ask yourself honestly if you are negating your passion to maintain the status quo in your relationship. Are you falling into the gender trap of always putting others before your own happiness?

Pushing Down MY Passion

I thought I could skirt around my own personal experience of putting aside my desires, but as I reflected on my own behaviours, particularly in the past, I realised the value of sharing them with you.

I'd had a passion for travel from a young age and for as long as I could remember I'd wanted to explore the world. I was captivated by travel books, TV programmes and films that featured travel and different countries. I remember when I was about ten years old, I bought my dad Michael Palin's book, *Around the World in 80 Days* for Christmas and before he had a chance to read it, I devoured it. I loved the candid adventures and knew that travel was what I wanted to do. The travel bug was coursing through my veins.

However, in my early 20s I fell hook, line and sinker in love. In fact, I didn't just fall in love, I was besotted, and it didn't matter that my partner wasn't interested in travel because I was in love! We had a child when I was 23 and when my son entered my life, happiness engulfed every atom of my being. I felt blessed.

I pushed down those wild wanderings that tugged at my heartstrings, I pretended travel wasn't important. I could say money was a factor and I could say that having a child was a factor, but in reality, it was neither of those things. Travel wasn't important to my husband and instead of answering the call of my own soul, I pushed my desire to travel down. I pretended my desires were frivolous and unimportant and sought happiness in my marriage. In fact, I bent myself out of shape for twenty years and focused on how I could make my husband and my marriage happy, thinking that would make me happy.

I thought...well if I cook, if I do this... if I say that... if I help with this...if I change this...then everything will be fantastic.

And yet it wasn't.

I felt like my personality was wrapped in a tight constricting mask and I couldn't take a deep breath.

Paulo Coelho states 'When we renounce our dreams and find peace we go through a period of tranquillity. But the dead dreams rot within us and infect our entire being. We become cruel to those around us, and then we direct this cruelty against ourselves' (1992, p.52).

Which is exactly where I was headed.

Anxiety, emotional breakdown, conflict and eventually divorce.

I broke my world apart and everything that I held dear because I felt choked.

It had taken me twenty years and a marriage breakdown to finally understand that I needed to focus on myself and put my own happiness first, and to realise that this was not a selfish act.

It took me twenty years to understand that love is gift, but any relationship is only as good as the relationship you have with yourself. If you are unfulfilled, unhappy or craving adventure, it doesn't matter how much you love someone dissatisfaction and resentment will seep in and taint the happiest of relationships.

What I wanted, lay buried in these ruins, like a tarnished jewel waiting to be unearthed to shimmer in all its glory.

How Do You Know What You Want?

The future is nothing less that the flowering of our inwardness.

– Rainer Marie Rilke

Trust your intuition, your gut.

Trust those feelings that won't go away.

The concept of intuition may seem whimsical. We've all been told by well-meaning friends to 'follow your intuition' but what does it mean? Does it mean anything?

In my mind, intuition is your inner compass. It's a direct link to your authentic self that we discussed in chapter 1. Imagine a cord of vibrating light connected to your core, sending feelers out into the world. When something is good for you, positive messages shimmy along the cord and give rise to feelings of joy and calm; and in contrast, when you do something that doesn't feel right, it usually gives rise to feelings of anxiety and unease, often centred in our gut. This is your intuition speaking.

When something is wrong, your gut will tell you so. Earlier in this book, I mentioned my first trip to Sri Lanka. I had an underlying disquiet and recurring unease in my tummy telling me things didn't feel quite right. My unease dissipated as I wandered through the temple alone and it was replaced by a soft sense of internal joy and a realisation that I would return to Sri Lanka and travel in a different way. This was my intuition speaking. The real me knew what was needed to nourish my soul.

I compare it to other times in my life when I knew what I was doing felt unequivocally right, for instance caring for my son as a baby – I threw away the baby manuals and went with my heart. When something is right, you know because you feel good, you feel an inner strength – it's your intuition, your inner compass, guiding you.

Also, trust those feelings that are recurring, those feelings that don't go away no matter how hard you try to dampen them down. I knew from a young age, that I wanted to travel, I didn't care how I did it or where, just that I wanted to travel. It was in my blood. I tried to hide those feelings, pretend they weren't important for years, but they kept boomeranging back. My heart knew and my intuition told me, but it took me many years to fully listen.

Is it really my intuition?

If you're sat there reading this, feeling somewhat sceptical about intuition that's understandable. Perhaps you've simply read a few blogs on solo travel and the thought has gotten you excited, and there's a niggling pulse of 'try it, try it...'

Well, I'd say, go for it – you won't know if you don't try it.

What Selfishness is...

We started this chapter by asking if solo travel was a sign of selfishness. I hope that I've helped to quieten that worry and dispel the myth. However, I do want to briefly mention what is selfish.

Selfishness is not considering your partner's thoughts and feelings.

Selfishness is holding on to your desires and leaving your partner out in the cold.

Happiness might be an inside job, and it's certainly not selfish to follow your own passions. However, it is selfish not to think about your partner's feelings and to go bullish through the world, expecting everyone else to fall in your wake.

When you make a commitment to someone, you have a responsibility to talk about what you would like to do. It's crucial to be upfront and honest so that you can discuss plans openly.

If the idea of talking to your partner about solo travel worries you, we'll explore how to broach the subject in the next chapter.

Journaling Prompts *(be honest with yourself)*

There are journaling opportunities throughout this book. Writing down your thoughts and feelings in this manner can 'be both a stress buster and your compass to understanding your emotions' (Psychologies, 2021).

Are there occasions when you push down your own desires? What desires are they? How does this make you feel?

How often do you put other's needs before your own? Why do you do this? How does it make you feel?

Do you sometimes put other's needs before your own and then feel bitter? How often do you do this?

What messages were you given in childhood about behaviour that is acceptable for a girl? How did this make you feel?

Why do you want to travel solo?

How does the idea of solo travel make you feel inside?

What stops you from travelling solo?

How do you think it would feel to tell your partner about your desire to travel solo? (If you haven't already.)

Activity – Create a Vision Board

Who looks outside dreams, who looks inside awakens.

– Carl Jung

Vision boards are a great way to visually represent your inner most desires and focus your mind on the things you really want in life. They are used to clarify, concentrate and maintain focus on those things that really matter to you.

The very simple act of visually representing your goals makes you much more likely to achieve them.

A vision board can:

- Help you tune in to your inner most desires.
- Keep you focused on your intention.
- Be used to state daily affirmations.

Several years ago, I was in a deep funk – I was at the point of having to start again in life. I felt sad, lost and not quite sure where to start. One evening, in despair, I grabbed all the magazines I could find and started cutting out pictures of the way I wanted my life to look and feel. There were travel pictures, pictures of laptops in a home office, pictures of a house in the sun, a large table outside with friends and family enjoying a meal, pictures of hearts and a scale to show balance and so on…

The very act of creating the vision board, was a tonic in itself; it focused my heart and helped to clear the mental fog and despondency. Although this was many years ago now, I remember the evening clearly because it was a mental turning point.

I pinned it to my wall. Sometimes I looked at it and consciously focused my intention on creating my vision. However, mostly, I forgot all about it, but this didn't matter, my intention was set.

Several years later, looking back at those torn out images I realised that I had created my vision – a freelance location independent lifestyle, which enables me to travel, a lovely partner and a house in Italy with a very big table where friends and family can join me for me meals.

There are no rules for creating a vision board, but I would suggest creating it in a quiet space where you will be undisturbed. Perhaps create a peaceful mood, by lighting a candle and burning some scented oils. Surround yourself with images, glue, coloured pens and a large piece of paper.

Take a few minutes to tune into your breathing and relax.

This is your time to have some fun.

Choose images that reflect your desires and stick them to your large sheet of paper. Don't try to rationalise or curtail your dreams – just go for it.

That's all there is to it.

If you want to stick it to the wall do so, alternatively, you may prefer to fold it up and put it in a drawer. It doesn't matter. The intention is set.

Let the magic unfold.

Chapter 4

BROACHING THE SUBJECT OF SOLO TRAVEL

We can use difficulties and problems to awaken our hearts.

– Pema Chodron

Are you dead set on wanting a solo travel adventure? Your soul is shouting out – get out there, get out there!

Perhaps you've been researching destinations, reading solo travel blogs in every spare minute, eyeing up cheap flights – your spirit is doing cartwheels in anticipation. Wow, I know this feeling!

But there's one small problem, you're struggling to find a way to tell your partner your plans. You've gone through imagined dialogues in your head and you're not sure what his reaction will be. Can you relate to this?

On many levels, this seems absurd, doesn't it? Let's face it, we're adults and we can do what we want. Surely, you just say 'hey… I'm going to book a solo holiday for next month, what you up to?' And yet, there are many reasons why it's not always that straightforward.

There are two things that are important to remember here:

1. Don't presume and underestimate your partner.
2. Communication is key.

Don't Underestimate Your Partner

When something is new, it's hard to predict how your partner may feel about it. Will they be excited for you and supportive? Will they freak out? Will they be jealous? I expect you'll have an idea of how they might react and perhaps you have played out many imaginary conversations in your mind. However, what I want you to remember is that our minds are wild! They concoct and run scenarios like we're watching a movie, with many different endings. It's so easy to fall into the trap of thinking your partner is going to react negatively when the opposite could be true.

Don't underestimate your lovely partner.

I learnt this valuable lesson at the end of a pandemic lockdown when I was itching to travel. It might be surprising that I'd struggled with broaching the subject of solo travel, especially as I'm writing a book on it. However, even though from the very first day I met my partner Scott, I'd made no secret about solo travel being a big part of my life and I'd been on previous trips, I found it difficult after two years of lockdowns to broach the subject when the time came.

Scott had just started a new full-time job and was finding it quite stressful, and despite spending the previous autumn in Italy together we hadn't had a holiday during the current year. I felt it would be very selfish of me to rush forward excitedly with my solo travel desires. My internal dialogue concocted a whole load of 'wow Jenny, you're so selfish wanting to leave your partner alone…you need to be around to be supportive…you need to ensure he feels happy…he will be so upset if you tell him…'

So, I kept my feelings to myself and didn't say anything. I tried to rationalise away my desire to travel. Needless to say, the feelings festered and surprise surprise I began to feel miserable and not at all like myself. I became anxious, a bit depressed and most unpleasantly I began to pick fault with Scott.

I fell neatly into the trap of trying to please him and thinking it was my responsibility to ensure he felt happy. My 'how to be the perfect partner' mode was shining bright, just like we discussed in the previous chapter. Yet, predictably, by side-lining my desire, I felt misaligned.

When I finally let it rip after a few weeks, he was very upset. Not because I wanted to go away without him, but because I'd held back and didn't talk to him about it. He felt sad that I'd tried to predict his reaction and even sadder that, I'd not given him the chance to show his love and respect for me. You see, by not sharing and thinking I knew what his response would be, I'd taken away the ability for him to listen to my heart about something that is very important to me. He wanted to support me and show his understanding, but I presumed I knew better.

Once we'd had this discussion, I immediately felt better, the space was cleared and we could start moving forward. What's more I began making plans for a trip to the Canary Islands.

So, please don't presume you know your partner's reaction, give him credit. It's so easy to waste your energy on imagined scenarios. Start with being open, it clears the way to get the conversation moving at the very least.

Communication is Key

In a relationship, your solo journey begins with communication. It's perhaps the most important factor, from start to finish.

I would also go as far to say, that communicating – talking and listening – is the crux of a successful solo travel adventure when you're in a relationship.

We are all unique and different things make us tick. What you like, might not be what your partner likes and that's cool. That's what makes people interesting. This is relatively easy to accept when the thing in question is something familiar. For example, my partner loves computer games and I'm afraid I simply don't get it but given that this is a hobby shared by millions of other people I accept it. However, solo travel is a little trickier because for many it's unchartered territory and unfamiliar. It can therefore be very difficult for someone who doesn't share that passion to get their head around it and understand why on earth you would want to do it.

Therefore, relaying your ideas and the reasons for wanting to travel solo is crucial in helping your partner understand why you want to do it and for alleviating any fears that may come up.

I recommend taking some time to reflect, using the journaling questions below. Writing down your reasons for wanting to travel solo will give you clarity and help you to clearly communicate your reasons to your partner.

He may not be immediately onside, cracking open a bottle of champagne – especially if this is the first time you've ever mentioned it, but once you put those wheels in motion you begin to open him up to the possibility. If you are met with an immediate negative reaction, remember that this is new and whilst you may have been thinking about solo travel for a while and have a clear understanding of why you want to do it, your partner has not.

If you come up against an immediate negative brick wall, recognise that this might be a defence mechanism and consider that he might be scared that this is a sign that your relationship is in trouble, nervous of the unknown or simply under the illusion that solo travel is for single people, not people in relationships. We will delve into all of this in detail in the next chapter.

I'd also recommend that before you talk to your partner, consider how you will react if you are met with negativity. Will you be angry, frustrated, clam up? Try to avoid this, it will set you off on the wrong footing. Consider a gentler approach, acknowledge your partner's anxieties, they are valid, but be clear and rational in what you want. How will you find a door in that wall?

Journaling Ideas

Writing can help to gain clarity on your reasons for wanting to travel solo so that you can explain them clearly to your partner.

Things to consider before you talk to your partner:

- Why do you want to travel solo?
- What does it mean to you?
- How does it make you feel?
- Where do you want to go and why?
- What do you think are the benefits of solo travel to you?
- What do you think the potential benefits are to your relationship?

Things you could do to alleviate negativity and open the space for progress:

- Reassure your partner of your feelings towards him.
- Give examples of other women who travel solo, show him blogs, books etc.
- Share this book with him.
- Involve him in the planning of the trip.
- Explore the idea of you each doing something independently.

Chapter 5

IT'S NOT WHAT COUPLES DO...

Life is about perspective and how you look at something... ultimately you have to zoom out.

– Whitney Wolfe Herd

Out of the potential challenges on your journey to solo travel, the notion that 'it's not what couples do' is perhaps the most powerfully ingrained and constraining for both partners.

Solo travel has taken off big time – it's one of the fastest growing styles of travel with more and more people every year taking the plunge. It's become widely accepted that travelling solo, especially as a single woman, is a pretty cool liberating thing to do.

However, when you present your idea of solo travel to your loved one, their reaction may be far from positive. I don't want to jump to any conclusions here, maybe they will weep tears of joy that you're going to embark on a new self-empowering solo journey, maybe they will recognise the merits of solo travel and support you from the moment you mention it. If that's the case, that is truly awesome. However, for many women, dealing with their partner's feelings on the matter of solo travel may not be quite so straight forward.

Some women I've talked to and interviewed during the process of writing this book, commented that their partners felt sure it was a sign that they were having doubts about their relationship, and one commented that her husband, almost on the verge of tears, asked whether she was leaving him. It took a lot of reassurance and explaining to help her husband understand her reasons for wanting to travel solo were nothing to do with how she felt about her marriage, but about fulfilling her own dreams.

I think it is reasonable to say that it's widely accepted these days that it's healthy for couples to have separate interests, different friends and to go on holiday with friends. However, the concept of solo holidays is still somewhat out there and massively misunderstood.

Unfortunately, it may not be just your partner's reaction that you have to deal with, but also your family and friends, who may not be too quick to applaud you. Instead, you may be met with raised eyebrows and concerned looks that your relationship must be on the slippery slopes. Why would you want to go off alone when you can travel with your partner, right?

Solo travel can be fabulous for the health of a relationship as we have already established in chapter 2, but whether your partner and friends will see it as a fabulous and burgeoning opportunity for relationship development is another matter entirely.

We (you and I, and all other women in relationships) need to flip the notion that solo travel equals relationship disaster completely on its head, it's outdated! It's so last century! It's time to create a new story. Let's begin with some relationship unravelling.

You may want to read and explore this chapter with your partner.

Relationship Unravelling: where do we gather our understanding of what a relationship is?

Relationships are actually simple...but the stories the mind maps around these simple relationships are incredibly complex, making it seem as if relationships are complex too.

– Oli Doyle

The world has changed, society has changed, how we live has changed and ideas about what constitutes an intimate relationship has thankfully evolved. However, in contrast our notion of how a couple should behave and what is or isn't acceptable behaviour is still often viewed through a very narrow lens. Solo travel, for many, has snuggly fit into the not acceptable category, until recently.

This narrow lens is shaped by a complex blend of cultural expectations, societal norms, historical factors and how you were raised as a child. In other words, we don't enter into our relationship as a blank slate. Instead, our expectations of how a partner should act and what should happen in our relationship is based on a whole cocktail of ideas developed over thousands of years which vary worldwide.

You only have to step back into history and look at how love is portrayed in art, books, and plays to remember that there are many variations in how relationships are constructed and how love is expressed. Take for example, medieval chivalry where suitors wooed their intended with serenades and poetry, or the formalised courting of the Victorians, or marriages as a transaction throughout history, and let us not forget naughty Louis XV's many socially accepted mistresses at the court of Versailles. It's so easy to criticise, pull apart and laugh at bygone forms of relationships, yet for some reason we are less likely to question contemporary notions of how to love. Instead, we accept them as the norm and the correct way to love.

Our dominating concept of love – the one that is portrayed time and time again in films from Hollywood to Bollywood, is the one where two people fall magically in love and live happily ever after. Yes sure, sometimes we belittle this formulaic romcom ideal, yet most of us believe in it to some extent (I hold my hand up high). The idea of finding our perfect partner, our soul mate is deeply ingrained into our psyche.

It's an ideal which is flaunted and constantly reinforced through popular culture – there's a whole genre of fiction, films, music and even computer games that are labelled as romantic. And let's not forget our beloved St. Valentine's Day; a day to celebrate the magic of love or perhaps if I am being cynical the obligatory social pantomime of love. How many valentine cards do you see with 'I can't live without you,' 'You're my other half' and consider how prevalent this is in our daily language of love, for example 'I need you, you complete me.'

Society celebrates romantic love like we have been whipped up into some frothy blissful state. We are sold the idea that when we find love, we have somehow made it, and with that notion comes the illusion that love should be enough to sustain our happiness. A state that is shared on social media as the epitome of bliss, reinforced by what our friends 'appear' to be doing and by what our parents did or didn't do.

Therefore, it's perhaps not so surprising that eyebrows are raised and partners question why their loved ones should want to venture forth alone, out of the cosy confines of the relationship, on a solo trip and why this may perpetuate or give rise to feelings of insecurity.

The idea of finding our perfect fit is beautiful, and there's no denying the universal feeling of wholeness that comes from falling in love, but any relationship is only as good as the relationship you have with yourself. If you are unfulfilled, unhappy or you simply crave adventure, it doesn't matter how much you love someone, dissatisfaction and resentment can seep in and taint the happiest of relationships.

To add to our formidable ideals around love, these days we may also expect a lot from our relationships. We may for example expect our partner to be a great lover, our best friend, co-parent and sometimes even our business partner (Solomon, A, 2017).

It's a beautiful idea isn't it, that of our partner being our everything, but how sustainable is it?

Your Relationship – Your Space

Where the myth fails, human love begins.

– Anais Nin

It's fascinating and somewhat disconcerting that for a subject that we seem to think we know so much about, relationships can actually be highly constraining and lead to much unhappiness.

Divorce currently hovers around 50% in the USA and 33% in the UK, and this does not account for the number of cohabiting and long-term intimate couples who decide to split up. It doesn't take too much of an imagination to consider that there's something in these figures that shows us that our IDEA of love and relationships must be flawed.

Unless I'm mistaken, I do not think that most couples start out thinking their relationship will end – of course not – hence that's why so many get married. Why would it be viewed as 'normal' to shell out money, sometimes thousands of pounds on a flamboyant wedding for there to be a 50/50 chance it could end in divorce?

Is it that all of these people are actually very poorly matched, and they were highly delusional when they got married? Yes maybe, in some instances. Is it that some couples simply grow apart? Again, yes sometimes.

Or is it that we're skating on thin ice with regards to what we expect from our partners and our relationships? Because let's face it, expectations can be rather HIGH!

A thought-provoking quote by Anais Nin declares 'Where the myth fails, human love begins.' The myth that one person can fulfil our every need, is just that, a myth. One that is easy to believe in when you are in the blossoming stages of a new relationship, but hard to maintain in the long run; hence why many relationships burn out, and why the cycle begins again.

Instead, perhaps it's time to put the myth aside and open ourselves to the many beautiful dimensions of love. Real love and loving the whole person.

A relationship is two people who choose to be together because they like and love each other. Within that relationship we have a choice. We can choose to wear blinkers and navigate our relationship from a know all perspective, following learnt patterns of behaviour, sticking with the loop and when something doesn't fit with 'what you know to be true' such as solo travel you could freak out, blame, sulk and argue; and if things don't fit for long enough perhaps, you'll grow bitter and break up.

Alternatively, we can choose to make a conscious decision to open ourselves up to learning about ourselves and our loved ones, we can say yes to unravelling our preconceived ideas that may have no bearing on who we really are, and we can acknowledge that deciding to make a commitment to someone is not the pinnacle, it's just the beginning of the journey.

When we choose to be open in this way, we are in control of creating a relationship that fits our individual personalities. Our relationship becomes a beautiful melting pot, in which you add the colourful spices; and when something new comes along, such as solo travel, you have the capacity in your heart and mind to approach it without the blinkers and add it to the fragrant pot of delight that is your relationship. When we approach a relationship in this way, it becomes a space in which to learn and grow, which enables our relationship to deepen and evolve over time.

Alexandra Solomon claims that 'loving like this is the work of a lifetime. As lovers we are never done, fixed or perfect. Nor would we want to be, as love thrives in the messy richness of me, you and us' (1997, p. 6).

Don't be mistaken, I'm not saying it's easy, ingrained thought patterns are never easy to break. It takes a commitment to say yes to the open road of possibility and it requires a commitment to consciously explore and acknowledge our baggage. However, when we do take this approach, we can banish the myth that 'people don't travel solo when they're in relationships.' Instead, we open ourselves up to the exciting and courageous possibility that relationships are not set in stone and that your relationship, be that a partnership or marriage, can be what you want it to be. It is yours to explore and it doesn't need to be like anyone else's you know.

And, if it's yours to explore we can flip outdated ideas about it not being cool to travel solo completely on its head and start again.

What If Solo Travel IS What Happy Couples Do?

Yes, that's right you read it correctly *solo travel is what happy couples do.*

If either you or your partner are struggling with the concept of solo travel, consider this – not so long ago, people thought I was crazy to want to travel solo, and I felt a bit weird claiming I loved it – and now look a whole industry has built up around it! Pop solo travel into Google and you'll be met by an avalanche of solo travel blogs, tour companies offering solo holidays and a bunch of magazine and newspaper articles bigging up the benefits. It's one of the fastest growing travel niches. So, like any social phenomena that was once regarded as normal or abnormal in the past, they change with time.

In addition, the world of travel has changed considerably and whilst we are still recovering from the impact of the pandemic, travel to many parts of the world is relatively straightforward and can be done on a budget. We can plan a vacation with relative ease and with increased internet connectivity stay in touch with loved ones from across the globe. Travel is significantly less daunting and much more doable.

And let's not forget that work has changed – more people than ever are embracing hybrid or remote workstyles, with some couples sharing not only a home but also their workspace. Never before has the division between work and home been so entwined, and whilst this brings many benefits, it also means some couples see a lot more of each other and with that there might be unforeseen challenges. It's only natural that you may crave a little alone time.

So, consider this – the perception of solo travel has changed, the world of travel has changed, work styles have changed – does it not therefore, make perfect sense that the perception of solo travel in a relationship is changing (or certainly on the verge of changing) and that actually solo travel IS what healthy happy couples do?

Say that to yourself 'solo travel IS what happy couples do!' Doesn't that feel great?

Keep saying it 'solo travel IS what happy couples do.' The more you say it and really feel it, the more it will seem very normal.

I can see it now:

Roll on five years into the future (maybe less) and as more and more couples jet off on their own solo adventures, it becomes the norm and very much a 'thing,' just like solo travel in general. There's a sea of change and a new way of thinking emerges. It is no longer regarded as sign that your relationship is in trouble but is symbolic of your solidarity and commitment to each other's personal happiness. It's symbolic of your trust and love. Solo travel IS what healthy happy couples do and in fact they do it because they are committed to growth, both personally and together. Why wouldn't it make perfect sense that you want to give your loved one the space to follow their dreams? In fact, why wouldn't you as partners and lovers encourage each other to travel solo so that your relationship can reap the rewards?

Reflect on that for a moment.

Journaling Prompts

Before we move on to the next section, here are some journaling prompts that you may find helpful. I suggest doing them with your partner. You could take turns to ask each other the questions and listen to each other's response. I mentioned the importance of communication in the previous chapter and by discussing these questions together, it can be a great way to open up the dialogue about your relationship and solo travel.

What perception do you have of female solo travellers? If this has a negative bias, why do you think it is the case?

How do you view people in relationships who want to travel solo? If this has a negative bias, why do you think it is the case?

What do you tell yourself about what a relationship is?

How much do you think you're influenced by: books, film & TV, social media, friends, family? How may it feel to let these ideas go?

What did you learn about relationships growing up?

Which of these learnt ideas are good for your relationship?

Which of these learnt ideas might be good to let go of?

What could you do to shift these ideas?

How important is it to you that your partner feels able to follow their dreams?

How important to you is it that your partner feels empowered and confident?

Activity

Our Relationship Space

It can be helpful to visually represent your relationship so that you can both see the type of relationship you want to create.

Get some paper and begin brainstorming under the following categories:

- Things you want to do together
- Things you want to do separately

Have fun with this, the sky's the limit. It's a great way to get the ball rolling and open the door to chat about your hopes and aspirations. There might be some surprises!

If any negative feelings come up, explore them. Ask 'why am I having a negative reaction?' and use some of the questions above to explore your feelings. Shining a light on negative reactions, allows us to unravel those thoughts. Also, sometimes the very act of voicing what makes you feel uncomfortable can help to ease the feeling and open the path forward.

Note: If you feel that you want to explore your relationship further, there are some excellent book recommendations in the resource section (see Appendix: Resources).

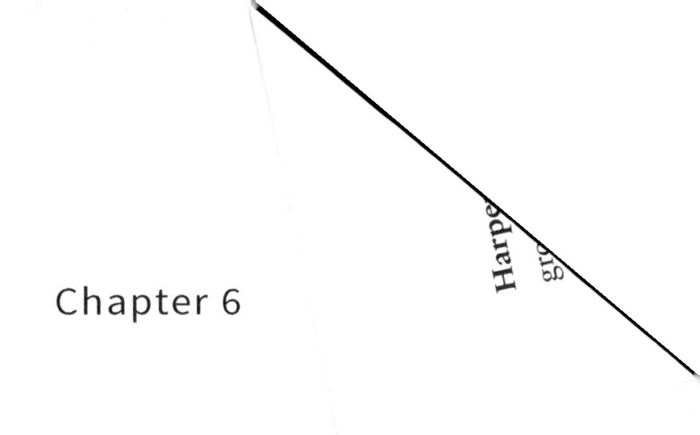

Chapter 6

SOLO TRAVEL IS WHAT HAPPY COUPLES DO

Tips to help you on your way

In the last chapter we flipped the antiquated belief on its head that solo travel doesn't fit into a relationship and established that solo travel is what happy couples do.

If you are struggling a bit with that idea, it's not surprising, this is new ground. So, let's continue along that path and look at some tips for helping you on your way.

Tip 1: Remember – You Are Not Alone

Whilst the idea of travelling solo while in a relationship might be new to you, you're definitely not alone. Here's a few statistics:

Lonely Planet – '60% of people who travel alone are in a relationship or married' (2018).

Solo Traveller – 'Women continue to travel solo more than men.' 47% of travellers with Overseas Adventure Travel are registered as 'solo'. An astounding 85% of these solo travellers are women (2022).

Harper's Bazaar – Flash Pack (a travel company specialising in group adventures for solo travellers in their 30s and 40s) did a survey 'on 2,000 people and found that 47 percent of Brits with partners want to go on a solo trip with the goal of trying new experiences and meeting like-minded people' (2019).

CNBC – 'The solo travel trend has grown exponentially over the past four years, according to Melissa DaSilva, North America president of The Travel Corporation's tour division' (2022).

Airbnb – have reported a marked increase in solo rentals.

Intrepid Travel – have reported that half of their guests are travelling by themselves which has led them to create the first ever solo tours.

Booking.com – now have a section on the website dedicated to providing solo travel advice due to the increase in demand of solo travel accommodation.

Tip 2: Be Your Own Power Couple

Whilst researching for this book, I read an article in the magazine *Brides* – I have to declare that this is not my normal bedtime reading but an article on 'power couples' caught my eye and got me thinking. Bear with me here!

Brides defined a power couple as 'a couple who both complement each other's strengths and support each other's individuality... and...when times are tough, they feel safe because they have a relationship motto of we'll figure this out together' (2021).

The media gives the label 'power couples' to those partnerships that appear to be solid and committed, whilst supporting each other's unique passions – Barack and Michelle Obama, Oprah and

Stedman, and Beyonce and Jay Z spring to mind. These couples appear to have each other's backs and strive to be there for each other.

If we strip this back and take away the celebrity masquerade, a power couple has nothing to do with having copious amounts of money or fame, it's about each individual in that relationship respecting and supporting each other's dreams and aspirations whilst maintaining a strong unit.

Can you imagine Barack saying to Michelle when she talks to him about taking a solo hiking vacation – 'nah Michelle, I'm not keen on that, the idea kinda freaks me out and makes me feel insecure' - I doubt it and I'm sure that Michelle would not stand for it. I think Barack would say 'yes babe, go for it – it will be good for you to have some space from my smelly socks and when I was president rants!'

So, be your own power couple – be each other's rock within a haven of love, where you both feel the unbound freedom to fly high, to follow your dreams and aspirations and then return to the safety and comfort of home knowing that you will be welcomed with open arms.

Tip 3: The Power of Presence

Love is the complete acceptance of
the other exactly as they are now.

– Oli Doyle

Disagreements within relationships are usually linked to the past or to the future in some way. They arise because of something our partners did or didn't do in the past or because of something that we are predicting might happen in the future.

Here are some examples:

Past example

In the past you didn't want to travel solo, what's changed? Why have you changed? = there must be something wrong, this makes me uncomfortable, this makes me very unhappy in the present = conflict.

Future example

I have this picture in my head of our future, it contains a lovely house, a big garden, kids, nights out…it doesn't include a picture of you travelling solo. This doesn't fit with my picture. This makes me feel uncomfortable and anxious = perhaps you will want to leave me, perhaps you don't really love me anymore = conflict.

When we use past references to define what we think our loved one should do in the present, or project into the future we are not dealing with the present situation. Instead, we are creating a story in our minds. We all do this, it's how our minds work – they are truly unruly! It's down to us to tame our minds, so our thoughts do not run rampant causing unnecessary anguish and conflict.

I don't know how long you have been with your partner, it could be 2 years, 10 years, 40 years; it doesn't matter. Regardless of the time span, it's normal for someone to change and want to try different things. However, this can be difficult for partners to accept, and disagreements can arise when one person wants to do something new, putting a chink into the normal routine of things.

Here's another example – Sarah and Ali

Sarah has been with Ali for 20 years. In that time, they had a child. Sarah and Ali's roles were clearly defined as parents, married couple, and hard workers. When their child went off to university, Sarah decided that she wanted to go on a solo vacation. Ali found the situation very challenging because Sarah had never wanted to travel solo before and she had always loved taking vacations with the family. When Sarah mentions her plans to Ali, it makes him feel very uncomfortable. He can't understand why Sarah suddenly wants to do this new thing. Sarah is hurt that Ali doesn't respect her desire to try something new.

In Ali's eyes Sarah is no longer playing her role properly. She isn't doing what she's always done, and this creates inner turmoil in his mind and conflict within the marriage.

Oli Doyle, in the book *Mindful Relationships* asks 'Is this true connection? Thinking about what you want someone to do and then feeling pleased when they do it, and upset when they don't, it doesn't seem particularly connected. It seems a bit selfish' (2019, p. 18).

As a rule, we do not do this because we are mean and want to restrict our partners, most people want the best for their loved ones. We do it because our minds like safety and control. Our minds like to keep us in our comfort zone, and when something comes along that rocks the boat and doesn't fit into that snug safety box, we feel uncomfortable. But as we know stepping out of our comfort zone is healthy.

By focusing on the present moment, without referring back or projecting forward we stop judging and feel happier and it becomes easier to accept change within your relationship. You create a dynamic free flowing space, which increases that beautiful sense of curiosity and excitement that we discussed in chapter 2. Where then is the fear? There is none (Doyle, 2019).

In contrast, when roles, expectations and shared experiences solidify in a constant battle to maintain equilibrium and not upset what always has been so, it can lead to the feeling of being boxed in and trapped. You may feel as though your partner is no longer your champion, but your keeper.

Does this mean that we ignore our past?

Not at all, it's always important to acknowledge the past and the impact it has on us today, our past experiences shape us and help us to understand our present selves, but at the same time it's important we don't get stuck there.

For guidance on being mindful, see Chapter 14 and Appendix: Resources.

Tip 4: Embrace the Bumpy Ride

When you reach that point of booking and setting off on a solo trip, it's important to recognise that it's highly likely that the rollercoaster of emotions will continue, for both of you.

Setting off is only the first step

You can plan, discuss, and take mindful steps but our emotions are unwieldy and rarely straightforward. Each day is a new dawning and each step along the way can bring new challenges - new niggling thoughts that spiral out of control or new pieces of baggage that we'd forgotten all about! You may think you've gotten over one hurdle and oh yea there's another one tapping at your solar plexus, creating unease and anxiety. Ahhhhhhhh! But remember, each hurdle is a chance to raise self-awareness. So, keep on going, embrace the bumpy ride.

I'm going to share with you, my partner's bumpy ride story because despite knowing that I loved to travel solo when he met me, the ride has not always been easy for him. Scott has never travelled solo himself and he's not a 'traveller.' However, despite the challenges, it has been an emotionally empowering journey; one where he's had to dig deep and analyse his own preconceptions of what it means to love someone. He and I have come out the other side stronger and our relationship is richer for it.

What follows is Scott's very honest account of his thoughts and feelings, and some of the challenges he has come up against whilst being in a relationship with a woman who loves to venture out into the world alone.

Scott's Bumpy Ride Story

I remember vividly when I first met Jenny of her passion and excitement for travel. She would avidly describe how she felt discovering new places with the wide-eyed verve of a child who's just received the best present ever. 'That's pretty cool' I thought. I've never been the travelling type myself (maybe this will change), but to have something that you're passionate about is a very attractive quality and says a lot about a person.

Never for a milli-second did I ever think Jenny's wanderlust would change and as a partner, your instinctive reaction is to wonder how you can support, embrace and nurture that desire. Equally, this was something completely new to me and I knew that it would challenge me emotionally and require me to adapt and evolve.

Jenny outlined, from her perspective, the benefits to both me and us; how it would give us space, that missing each other would be healthy and that it would give me time for self-reflection and to pursue my own interests.

So, laying any scepticism aside, I entered into the relationship with my eyes fully open. No-one wants to see the person they love stagnate because their soul is not being nourished due to the death of a passion, and quite frankly Jenny was not going to change for anyone!

However, all this idealism is all well and good but it's not so easy to be intrinsically enthusiastic when you're the one who's left behind!

I remember telling myself as I prepared for Jenny's 6-week trip that there are millions of people for whose life this is the norm – pilots, oil-rig workers, journalists – the list goes on. Me? I am a college maths tutor who has spent my entire adult life, from the age of 17 in long term relationships based around the societal norm of 'you live together, you do couple stuff and that's that.' In almost 33 years I had only been apart from a partner for a week at the most and yet here I was, with a partner I did not live with at the time, who was about to go off adventuring without me. To try to detail the entire experience of being the one left at home would take a long time, so I shall try to be succinct.

Human nature, especially if you're not used to being with someone who loves travelling is to initially feel a sense of loss. Missing the person you love can manifest itself in many ways and going through the whole plethora of emotions is a difficult process.

I'd never thought of myself as an insecure person and prior to Jenny leaving I thought I was mentally prepared, but I was not. It was hard. I was taken by surprise by the insecurity that enveloped me and I'm sure I'm not unique in saying that the dominant emotion of insecurity is the very thing that stops many people from supporting their partner's solo travel in the first place. The fear of 'what if they meet someone else' devil is hard to shake, however childish it may seem.

However, it's what you do to overcome that fear and how you recognise it as just that, fear, that's important.

I believe we learn a lot about ourselves when we are placed in unfamiliar scenarios. In this instance, my ingrained belief system was being questioned. I needed to open myself up to a broader less constrictive view, but it was difficult and draining at first. The knee jerk reactions and the desire to protect oneself are very dominant forces.

It took nearly 3 weeks for me to finally get to grips with everything and then I almost changed overnight. I realised that you could visit the well of love within you and find a hidden spring that lifts you up and pushes you toward the sunshine. The self-pity, the scared and worried soul who had been trying to reason with himself in the 'man cave' was gone and here was a happy man. A man who actually did embrace his partner's passion, who felt supportive, who wanted to be more involved and encourage Jenny to relish in her freedom and the beauty of her surroundings.

I felt like a person who had just vanquished their evil doppelgänger, ready to put right all of the wrongs his malignant twin had done. I was ready to greet my love upon her return with an open happy heart and to impart my true uncluttered emotions that I had missed her terribly and loved her deeply.

What would I say to other people who find the idea of their partners wanting to travel alone difficult?

That it might be difficult, and you may have to face many demons. You may worry about your partner; you'll miss your partner, and you may feel insecure and vulnerable. However, above all else you will also feel content that your partner is doing something that makes them genuinely happy.

It's important to understand that even though you are not there, you ARE there, you are together. You can share in the experience through photos, messages, and conversations. You can spice up your love life by thinking of new and inventive ways to be intimate.

I think it's also crucial to recognise that it takes time to adapt, but it can only add depth, spice, and love to your relationship.

I've also learned that overcoming these things, in no matter how small a measure is both a rewarding victory and a liberating experience.

Tip 6: Encourage Passion

Passion is energy. Feel the power that comes from focusing on what excites you.

– Oprah Winfrey

We discussed in chapter 1 the importance of doing things that rock your heart and make your spirit dance, whether that's solo travel or something else. Obviously, this is not a one-way thing. Having a passion or multiple is healthy for both partners for two key reasons:

Firstly, how can you relate to someone else having a passion, like solo travel, if you don't have one yourself? My love bug's passion is motorbikes, and do I get it? No not really. I get the feeling of freedom that he says biking gives him, but I'd prefer to get that through travelling rather than whizzing along at 70 + mph on a big scary motorbike. The point is, passions can be anything – art, football, cooking, playing music… anything, and it's not really until you have one that you can relate to someone else's.

Secondly, when you have a passion that feeds your inner cup of bliss, it's good for your overall wellbeing. It gives you the internal reassurance that you are the master or mistress of your happiness and that you don't need your loved one to make you happy. You come to your relationship whole, and you therefore give the best of yourself.

If you or your partner are holding onto the romantic notion, that you are two halves slotted together to make a whole and all you need is each other, one person's passion can seem like a slap in the face to the other! Why? Because it will seem like they don't 'need' you quite as much as you need them; so shake that idea to the ground and find a passion!

Tips for finding a passion:

- Revisit something you loved to do but stopped for some reason.
- Try something you've always wanted to do.
- Try lots of new things to discover a few you may love.

Tip 7: Imagine Your Relationship as A Flourishing Garden

A relationship or a marriage is not a finished product. It's a garden to nurture, in which to play, experiment and flourish. Imagine your relationship garden, the individual sunflowers proud and strong with striking yellow heads and the glorious aromatic clematis entwining with enduring love. Like all good gardens care and attention is needed for optimum beauty. All the plants need space to grow, and just like you and your partner, crowding can result in a loss of vitality; so, remember to prune away the deadheads and unnecessary foliage!

And what's more don't forget you need a good dollop of poop! It goes a long way to creating strong, healthy flowers. Poop – yes there's always poop, isn't there? – it's the challenges that life throws at you. The pain, the worries, the hurdles, that in the end make you stronger or more resilient. If your partner declares that they want to travel solo for a month, it could initially be a big dollop of poop. Initially smelly, and worry worthy, but in the end, it'll make your roses all the sweeter and your relationship all the more satisfying.

There is no other garden like yours, its distinctive and characteristic of all the hard work you have put into it. You can add new flowers and prune it occasionally, but you can also just sit back, relax and enjoy your creation in the present moment.

Chapter 7

TRUST

Love cannot live where there is no trust.

– Edith Hamilton

Trust is the foundation for all relationships. Trust means that you feel safe and secure with your partner, and you are confident that they will not hurt you. Trust allows you to be vulnerable and real, making your relationship a place of solace (Psychology Today, 2018).

To feel that you are fully trusted, and to trust back is crucial and as discussed in chapter 1 solo travel can be a way to further deepen trust in your relationship.

However, we are all at different stages with trust and it takes time to develop – sometimes years depending on a variety of personal factors including past experiences.

If trust presents itself as an issue for you, it's certainly not a reason to avoid solo travel. Quite the opposite, it presents an opportunity to look at those issues with your partner and work through them. Only good can come from tackling trust issues head on.

It's also important to note that when we are discussing trust, we are not only talking about the partner who wants to travel solo but both partners. It's easy to focus on the person who is venturing out into the world alone, but trust issues can go both ways and it's just as likely that the person who wants to travel solo may struggle with trusting the partner who is left home alone. In other words, just because you love the idea of travelling solo, it doesn't necessarily mean you have no trust issues. There have been times when I have been away and all of sudden, I start concocting a whole scenario whereby my partner has had enough of my gallivanting, and he finds someone else – just like that!

As a starting point, it's a good idea to figure out where you sit on the trust scale.

The Trust Scale

Look at the following statements and decide which applies to you. I'd recommend working through them as a couple. You may find you are individually at different stages and this exercise will help you to identify that and start the conversation about trust.

Which statement is true for you:

1. I trust my partner wholeheartedly.
2. I have no reason not to trust my partner, but I feel insecure at the prospect of them solo travelling or being separated from them for a prolonged period.
3. I have valid reasons not to trust my partner.

1. I trust my partner wholeheartedly.

If you trust your partner unreservedly, that's great. It's likely that the time apart will continue to deepen your connection and further solidify the trust and security you already have.

Tip: although trust doesn't present a particular concern for you, you may still find it helpful to continue work through the rest of this chapter in preparation for your solo trip.

2. I have no reason not to trust my partner, but I feel insecure at the prospect of them solo travelling.

If you have no reason not to trust your partner, but you feel insecure at the thought of a sustained absence, this is understandable and common. You love your partner and as we discussed in the Chapter 5, *It's Not What Couple's Do...*, when something unusual comes along to change your normal routine it's natural to feel a little unnerved.

However, it's also important to remember to look at the bigger picture. This situation is a really good opportunity to deepen your trust and grow as a couple. Imagine how liberating it will feel to fully trust your partner.

I liken it to a comfort zone, presently the level of trust you have developed is within a set of circumstances that are familiar to you. Perhaps you have been together for a number of years, and you've built that level of trust between you. However, when you are presented with the idea of solo travel, you're having to step out of that comfort zone of trust and so it feels uncomfortable. It's normal to feel this way, but like all comfort zones, when you step through the fear, emotional expansion occurs, and you can't imagine going back. It's like stepping out of a swimming pool of trust into a vast sea of trust.

Tip: to help you and your partner feel more confident about solo travel, I'd recommend that you continue to work through this section including the journaling/discussion prompts, ground rules for solo travel and the practice of presence.

3. I have valid reasons not to trust my partner.

Okay, so you have valid reasons not to trust each other, perhaps past experiences have tarnished your trust. Where do you go from here?

Firstly, it's important to recognise that trust takes time to build, it's not an overnight job and if you're holding your hand up and identifying that trust is an issue, you're taking a courageous step towards strengthening trust and building a relationship with a more secure base.

The feeling of not being trusted or not trusting is very unpleasant and if you allow it to, it can seep into many aspects of your relationship life, rotting it from its core. A lack of trust can result in problems with intimacy, negativity, insecurity, anxiety, distress and loneliness. It is therefore crucial to work on any trust issues.

The following pages set out some very useful tips for working on trust, but I want to point out that this chapter is about dealing with trust in relation to travelling solo, and not relationship trust in general. If you feel that a lack of trust is limiting your relationship and having a detrimental effect on how you feel about yourself and your relationship, you may find it helpful to work with a trained counsellor or work through a relationship self-help book that is specifically designed for relationship coaching (Please see Appendix: Resources).

Trust and Communication Go Hand in Hand

Without communication there is no relationship. Without respect there is no love. Without trust there's no reason to continue.

– Karen Salmansohn

Communication is fundamental to establishing trust. Effective communication lays in the ability to talk openly and to listen with an open heart.

When you listen to your partner fully, without judgement and with compassion, it is a gift; you are being a true friend. As D. Augsburger put it so perfectly, 'being heard is so close to being loved that for the average person, they are almost indistinguishable' (1982).

From my own perspective, knowing that Scott listens and respects my love of solo travel is a demonstration of his love. I know that despite his apprehensions and waves of insecurity, he hears me; and the fact that he has been willing to work through his insecurities has been one of the greatest gifts of love that I have experienced.

Talk openly and gently about your worries and doubts. Sometimes just the simple act of voicing your concerns helps with understanding them and sometimes just stating your worries can feel like a weight has been lifted, and you can see a way forward.

I like to imagine a tightly woven yarn ball of worries, and by loosening and unravelling the yarn, you can examine the textures and colour in more detail. Then when you wind the yarn back into a ball, looser this time, with greater flexibility, you have a more in-depth understanding of the individual strands.

The following prompts could be used for journaling or alternatively, they could be used to start the discussion on trust.

Journaling/Discussion Prompts

Do you carry some old wounds that influence your current thoughts?

What feelings arise when you remember old wounds?

What do you lose from not trusting?

What do you think it would feel like to trust your partner unreservedly?

Does your partner trust you? How does this make you feel?

What feelings arise when you consider a prolonged absence such as solo travel?

What would help you feel more secure during a prolonged absence?

Do you trust yourself? How does this make you feel?

Trusting Yourself

As soon as you trust yourself, you will know how to live.

– Goethe

The last journaling question may not seem as important as the rest, but in fact it's perhaps the most important. When we trust ourselves, we have faith that we are living in accordance with our own standards and ethics. How can you expect someone else to trust you if you don't trust yourself?

There have been times in my life, where my personal standards and level of integrity were low and in return I was treated poorly. I am not proud of this, but I'm also not ashamed. It was a life stage that I needed to go through to figure out my own self-worth. I did a lot of emotional work and realised that to get the best out of life, I needed to set my standards high both in terms of how I wanted to live and how I wanted to be treated by others. When I entered my current relationship, it was clear in my mind about the type of relationship I wanted – one based on mutual respect, trust and love – and trusting myself was fundamental.

When you trust yourself, you know that you won't be unfaithful, because it would be incongruent with your principles and personal integrity. From this point of inner trust, you build an inner strength that informs how you interact with your loved one and feeds into your relationship as a whole.

However, nothing is ever plain sailing, is it? Emotions are like whirlwinds, they come at you when you least expect them even when the air feels calm. We're humans after all. There have been times when both Scott and I have been at the mercy of nagging trust issues…an annoying worry here or a soaring out of control mind burp there…! However, despite finding those times upsetting, it really helped to have a strong sense of personal trust. It enables you to interact with confidence and reassurance.

When we trust ourselves, we project it out into the world. You become your own best friend, you know what is right for you and you know how to live in a way that is right for you. You'll attract people that are good for you and furthermore, avoid those people that undermine your self-trust.

Ground Rules for Solo Travel

Ground rules are very useful and a good way to establish trust before you embark on a solo trip. They enable you to have a shared understanding of what you expect from each other whilst you are apart, and they provide reassurance that you are both agreeing to work in the same direction.

Ground rules could include:

- Your communication strategy
- Boundaries

Your Communication Strategy

How often do you both need to communicate and how?

I've mentioned communication a lot throughout this book, but I can't emphasise enough how important it is. It can make or break a solo trip. It's therefore a really good idea to establish how often you want to communicate and by what means. Not only is communication important for trust, it's also reassurance that you are safe.

You may feel it's a little over the top to plan your communication, but it's so easy to create undue worry when your communication style isn't aligned. For instance, it might be that one partner is perfectly happy with an occasional chat and doesn't feel the need for regular contact, but to the other partner who needs frequent update texts in order not to worry, this could create unnecessary stress.

As you get into the swing of things, no doubt you'll find your own rhythm naturally, but it's a really good idea to have those initial discussions so that you're both on the same page.

Our requirements for communication can also vary depending on what we're doing. It's easy to forget about communicating if you're busy, but if your partner's waiting to hear from you, alarm bells could start ringing.

On a trip to Malaysia, with an 8 hour time difference, I arrived feeling very tired after the long flight and I also had some work deadlines which were making me feel quite stressed. On arrival at the apartment in Kuala Lumpur, I attempted to work, but was much too tired so went to bed. The combination of jet lag and stress resulted in a few days of interrupted sleep, waking up at strange times, working under pressure and dozing off. I barely noticed the days flick by and despite texting Scott on arrival to say I'd landed, I sent very few additional texts in those first few days. This got us off to a rocky start. He didn't realise the extent of the work I had to do, and the lack of communication fed into his insecurities.

In hindsight, we both realised that we should have put down some ground rules with regards to communication and I certainly should have stressed the jet lag and work challenges that I was having. It would've saved a lot of undue worry. (I also learnt on that trip to at least give myself a few days breathing space before doing any kind of work after a long-haul flight!)

3 Tips for Smooth Communication:

Frequency – how often do you both want to communicate? For the less worry prone, a quick text once a day may suffice, but for others regular updates throughout the day might be required. If you discuss this in advance, you won't start off on the wrong foot and worry each other unnecessarily.

Method – how do you want to communicate? It's important to feel satisfied with the method of communication you're using, perhaps for instance you need to see and hear your partner, and texts simply will not cut it. Therefore, discuss whether you will text, chat, video call, have online meetings or a combination of all four.

Unavailable – leaving your phone behind for the day? Tell your partner! You don't want to create unwarranted worry by not responding to a text for several hours because you simply went to the beach for the day.

Sometimes it's the simplest of things that make all the difference, but if they aren't arranged clearly beforehand it's easy to set someone off on an anxiety ridden trajectory of worst-case scenario mental imagining.

Boundaries

Establishing boundaries is a great way to foster trust prior to a solo trip. When we set boundaries, it allows us to discuss what we are comfortable with and what we are not comfortable with. Boundaries enable us to create reassurance (Relate 2022).

I'd recommend you start with a piece of paper and have two columns labelled:

- I'm comfortable with…
- I'm not comfortable with…

You can then discuss comfort levels in relation to activities, types of accommodation, length of stay, locations, and anything else that you feel is important. You may not feel the need to discuss all of these, it's up to you.

For example, it might be that your partner is comfortable with you joining an organised wine tasting tour in Paris, but not so comfortable with you going on a Meetup bar crawl in Madrid. Or, for instance your partner might be comfortable with you going away for one week, but not two.

Expect to have differences in opinion, you can't force your partner to feel the same way as you or to totally understand, but it's likely through discussion that you can meet somewhere in the middle.

And remember this is just a starting point, a way to build trust and reassurance on your first step towards solo travel. It's not set in stone, and as you both become more comfortable with solo travel you can expand those boundaries and be much more fluid.

	Activities	Locations	Length of stay	Types of accommodation
I'm comfortable with...				
I'm not comfortable with...				

For ground rules to work you need to:

- **Be true to your word** – don't say things you won't stick to. How can you build trust if you don't act on what you said?
- **Be honest** – don't say things that don't reflect how you feel. Telling lies, even small ones undermine the development of trust.
- **Communicate effectively** – find a time to talk when you both feel relaxed. It's important not to shout or shut down the conversation when you hear something you don't like. The aim is to find a mutual level of agreement.
- **Remind yourself** – when you're away from home, it can be easy to get lost in the moment. Remind yourself about what you have agreed to and stick with it.

Review Your Ground Rules

Once you've set your ground rules, it's a good idea to set aside some time during the trip to review and re-evaluate how you are both feeling.

Reviewing them this way, may seem strange and more like a work project than relationship development, but it helps to ensure that you are both still on the same page and to stop any unexpressed feelings from festering.

While you are on your solo trip, make time to check in with each other and review your ground rules. Perhaps you could arrange a zoom meeting.

You could discuss:

1. What feels okay?
2. What doesn't feel okay?
3. Do you need to change anything?

Trusting in the Present

In Chapter 6 we discussed the importance of being present. Often, when trust comes up as an issue, it's because we are looking into the past at something that reduced our level of trust, or we are projecting into the future and visualising something that might happen to cause us pain.

For example, perhaps a previous or current partner cheated on us, or we witnessed our parents cheating and although the hurt caused by the indiscretion was in the past, it can deeply affect how we trust in the present. Our hearts remember the pain it caused and quite rightly we want to avoid feeling like that again at all costs. Consequently, we may project into the future, imagining our partner cheating and how horrible this would feel.

It's, therefore, only natural that we want to protect ourselves and avoid a situation where this might happen which explains the temptation to strike up the barriers against solo travel.

The problem is when we live in this way, flipping from the past to the future, we're story making. It's tiring and anxiety producing, and without developing a deeper level of trust, we will never really get the relationship that we truly deserve. In contrast, when we bring our focus to the present moment, our minds quieten and as we turn inwards, we welcome the very real infinite ocean of love that is within us right now and from there, we can act from a place of love, rather than a place of fear. And when we act from a place of love, we can move forward.

Liam and Maria's story

Liam and Maria have been together for 5 years. Liam's previous partner cheated on him which caused him a great deal of pain. He has built up a level of trust with Maria and feels happy and confident in their relationship. However, when Maria decides she wants to go on a two-week holiday by herself, alarm bells begin ringing for Liam. He remembers the hurt caused by his previous relationship, and although he trusts Maria, his memory of the previous emotional pain causes him to feel anxious and worried at the mere thought of Maria going away. He begins projecting into the future that Maria will meet someone new whilst she is away...and his thoughts spiral out of control.

Liam sits with this worry for a while. It causes him to be short with Maria, and although he doesn't want to, he starts feeling agitated with her; the atmosphere in the house is tense and unpleasant.

When Maria finally confronts Liam, he's already built up the picture in his head whereby Maria cheats on him as though it's really going to happen and he lashes out, pointing out that if Maria goes away, she'll probably cheat.

Understandably Maria feels very upset by the accusations as Liam has no reason not to trust her, and she points this out. After a heated discussion, Liam realises that he's acting on past pain and feels upset that his past is haunting his present ability to trust Maria. They realise that in order to move forward, they need to work together on building trust. Liam also understands that he needs to be much more aware of habitual thought patterns, which have no bearing on reality and so decides to find out about mindfulness.

See Chapter 14, Practicing Presence, for guidance on how to be more for mindful.

Chapter 8

SAFETY

A ship in a harbour is safe,
but that is not what ships are built for.

– John Shedd

For many prospective solo female travellers and their partners, safety is a major worry and can halt travel plans in their tracks. The fear that something bad may happen to you is understandable and unfortunately there's no getting away from the fact, that there is a risk and that yes as a woman, you are sadly more at risk than a man. However, it's also crucial to put this risk into context and look at the bigger picture.

Firstly, reports in the media of female tourists being the victims of random acts of violence, rape and even murder are startling and abhorrent, but like all news stories they focus on a minority of occurrences and unfortunately perpetuate the notion that the world is riddled with people wanting to cause you harm; making solo travel seem like an incredibly dangerous and irresponsible pursuit. When in reality, thousands upon thousands of women travel alone to all parts of the world every year, without incident and have a fantastic experience.

Secondly, crime can happen anywhere, and criminals exist in every country in the world. My home city in the UK is Nottingham and it's repeatedly in the news for knife crime, drug related violent crime and I recently read about the increase of drink spiking in bars. Do I avoid venturing out alone in case something happens to me? No. Instead, I do things to minimise my risk such as avoiding certain areas when it's dark, arranging transport in advance if I go out at night and not accepting drinks from strangers.

If we avoid doing things because of potential risk, we wouldn't leave our houses, our city or our country.

You have a choice to make - do you want to live in fear and create a self-imposed prison of what ifs? Do you want to limit yourself on the basis of your gender? Or do you want to embrace life to the fullest and live in a way that brings you joy, whilst being aware of risks and knowing how to minimise them?

I know which option I choose.

There are many things that you can do on a practical level to stay safe whilst you're on a solo trip.

In this chapter, we'll explore:

- How to reduce partner anxiety around safety.
- How to minimise risk as a female solo traveller.

How to Reduce Partner Anxiety Around Safety

We all know how it feels to worry about a loved one. It's a horrible gut churning feeling and no matter how much rationalising you do, worry can seep in and ruin a perfectly good day. I know, because I am the world's best when it comes to worrying about my loved ones!

As part of your pre-trip planning, I recommend the following:

1. Agree on your communication strategy.
2. Discuss your boundaries.
3. Review the 'Minimising Risk' list together.

1. Agree Your Communication Strategy

We talked about having a communication strategy in the previous chapter, Trust, and it's equally as important here in helping to ease partner anxiety about your safety.

As part of your pre-trip planning, it's advisable to discuss your communication strategy – see previous chapter.

2. Boundaries for Safety

In the previous chapter, we also discussed that using boundaries can help with establishing and working towards a higher level of trust. In this chapter, we will use boundaries to alleviate partner anxiety in relation to safety.

By creating clear safety boundaries, we reassure our partners that we will not do activities or visit locations that place us in danger.

The key point of doing this activity, is not to set limitations, but to have an open discussion about safety. How do you know if you don't discuss it? It's easy to presume that just because you regard an activity as safe, that your partner also does, but this may simply not be the case.

You could either do this activity before a trip you already have planned or as an opener for discussing safety and solo travel in general.

Get a piece of paper and have two columns labelled:

- Safe
- Unsafe

Next, discuss activities and places that you regard as either safe or unsafe for you as a solo traveller. For example, I think most people would regard a visit to an art gallery as relatively safe, whereas some may feel that going on a solo hike in a new location is less safe.

Expect to have differences in opinion, what can seem safe to one person, might not to another. If something comes up as an activity that you really want to do, but it makes your partner feel concerned, negotiate, and meet in the middle. For example, rather than setting off on a hike alone, arrange a guided tour or do your research and choose a hike that is popular with others, so that you know you'll not be walking alone for miles (I'd recommend this anyway for any solo female traveller).

3. Review the *'How to Minimise Risk'* List Together

If your partner is worried about safety, read through the next section together. It's the perfect chance to talk about safety and reassure each other that safety is at the forefront of your planning.

How to Minimise Risk as A Solo Female Traveller

The extensive list below of safety strategies may at first glance seem quite alarming and put you off travelling altogether! However, most of these points are common sense and I expect for some, you'll roll your eyes and mutter 'yes of course,' and then there will be others where you think 'hmm I'd not thought of that, good point!'. I'd recommend reading through them even if you are a seasoned traveller as it's always good to have a refresher.

I've categorised safety into the following:

- Research
- Using your phone
- Personal safety
- Property safety

Research

1. Do your research

Don't book a flight and head off without doing a bit of research into your location. By researching you are armed with the facts about a country, so that you can make an informed choice about whether to go there and what precautions to take.

Most governments have a website that gives travel advice for every country in the world in relation to weather, natural disasters, political climate, civil unrest, the covid situation and terrorist threat. Most also provide the level of risk associated with visiting that county.

However, please remember to read the advice with a sense of perspective. The government is legally obliged to inform you about the potential risk. That does not mean that it is a common occurrence or that you should be put off from travelling there, but it can alert you to taking sensible precautions.

Some governments, including USA and Australia, offer a service where you can register your travel plans to receive up to date travel advisories. In addition, you can register your travel plans and length of stay, so that if you do not return within a specified period of time, it will alert the government to find you.

USA www.step.state.gov (SMART Traveller Enrolment Program)
Australia www.smartraveller.gov.au (Smart Traveller)
UK www.gov.uk (for travel advice)
Canada www.travel.gc.ca/travelling/advisories (for travel advice)

2. Check out cultural norms and dress codes

To avoid offending the locals, it's always a good idea to read up on cultural norms and acceptable dress codes. For example, if you're going to a Muslim country, it's not a good idea to pack a load of shorts and skimpy dresses, you'll not only stand out like a sore thumb, but it would be regarded as very offensive.

Things are a little different in tourist resorts, though generally speaking if you're planning on venturing out alone it's important to be mindful of dress codes to avoid unwanted attention. Let's face it as a foreign woman alone, you're already going to stand out. Make an effort not to attract additional attention.

Using Your Phone

3. Keep your loved one updated

Yes, you might be a grown-up independent woman, who doesn't normally inform her partner of her every move, but don't be stubborn when it comes to safety. It's a good idea to keep your partner in the loop with regards to your accommodation and where you're going each day.

Ensure someone expects to hear from you every day, that way if anything happens to you, loved ones will be alerted quickly and can raise the alarm.

Most places have Wi-Fi these days, so it's no great shakes to send a quick WhatsApp message.

4. Keep your 'go to' phone numbers safe

Keep your go to friends' and family's numbers and email addresses written down somewhere separate from your phone and purse, in case you lose or have them stolen. It's a horrible feeling to lose your phone and then realise that all your essential information is within that one device. Don't put yourself in this situation.

Consider having a backup phone. I use my old phone as a backup. It has my essential numbers in it, and I use it when I don't want to take my expensive phone out with me.

5. Emergency numbers

We all know our home emergency numbers, but do you know it in the location you're in? No? Google it before you cross the border and save it. In the UK it's 999 and Europe 112.

6. Don't let your phone battery die!

Avoid letting your phone battery die at all costs. We all know how quickly batteries can drain, especially if we're using Google Maps a lot, but remember your phone is your best friend. If anything happens to you, it's your lifeline. Have you seen those survival programmes where the presenter in alarmed overtones claims '… and if they hadn't been using their phone to take lots of pictures, their battery wouldn't have died, and they would've been able to call for help rather than being stuck out in the rainforest for 3 days without food…'? Don't be that person.

If your battery is low, put it on battery saver mode and avoid using it unless you need to.

Always take advantage of wall plugs to charge your phone and consider buying back up batteries.

Personal Safety

7. Don't post on social media until you've left

If you plan to share travel photos on social media, avoid sharing whilst you are still at the location, it can put you at risk. Yes, of course you want to Insta the fabulous hotel you're staying in but wait until after you've left and then make everyone jealous.

8. Don't look lost

Try not to look lost, it makes you an easy target.

Admittedly, this is easier said than done if you've just arrived somewhere new! However, if you check out your route in advance and know some key landmarks this will help you feel and look more confident. If you start to feel lost, avoid standing on a street corner with your phone out peering at Google maps, instead find somewhere where you are less conspicuous such as a café or a hotel.

If it's night-time, it goes without saying that you need to be extra careful or ideally have pre-booked transport.

9. Be aware of your surroundings

As a solo woman traveller, you need to be aware of your surroundings and any people that might be targeting you. If you usually listen to music whilst walking, I'd suggest that you avoid doing so in a foreign location so that you can hear what's going on around you.

Useful questions to ask yourself:

Is someone walking too close to me?

Has anyone been walking behind or next to me for several minutes?

Is a car/moped slowing down near me unnecessarily?

Don't be paranoid but do be conscious of your surroundings. Pay attention to your intuition, if something doesn't feel right, best to remove yourself rather that test whether you were right.

If in doubt, pop into a shop or a café for a few minutes until you feel confident the person or vehicle has moved on.

10. Choose your smiles carefully

Nobody wants to come across as the unfriendly tourist, but be aware that smiling, making eye contact and being polite to people, particularly men, can bring unwanted attention.

If people are hassling you, don't acknowledge them. Yes, it can feel rude, but even a 'no thank you' can be regarded as a sign that you understood and an invitation to carry on. If it feels rude, remind yourself that actually they are being very rude by pestering you.

Keep your eyes forward, shoulders back and walk purposefully.

11. Arrive during the day

Plan to arrive at your destination during the day. There is nothing worse than arriving at an airport in the early hours, getting into a taxi and travelling along dark unfamiliar roads.

Check your flight arrival time and plan how you are going to get to your accommodation.

These days if I'm travelling long haul solo, I pre-book and pay for a taxi through booking.com. It's tracked, it's secure and I know that when I arrive there will be someone waiting with my name on a board.

I didn't use to book a taxi because I thought it was an unnecessary expense, but I've realised that following long-haul flights I'm not at my sharpest and that's when I'm most likely to make a mistake. For example, I once arrived in Bali, went to the airport ATM, withdrew some money and didn't wait for my card to be returned – not a great start to a holiday! Therefore, I book a hotel close to the airport for my first night and book a taxi. It gives me time to adjust and for my wits to return.

12. Getting around

When it comes to getting around, my personal ethos is to do as the locals do and if you're not sure ask the locals.

Public Transport - I'm personally a big fan of public transport and choose it when I can. It's usually the cheapest option and as a woman travelling solo, I prefer safety in numbers as opposed to jumping in a taxi.

It goes without saying that you must check timetables, you don't want to be stranded because you missed the last bus!

Don't presume you can book trains and long-distance buses online. In some countries you still need to go to the train or bus station to prebook.

If you're not sure whether the public transport in the country you're visiting is safe, check with the locals or in your hotel as they will know best.

Rideshare

Avoid hailing random taxis, and use rideshares such as Grab and Uber. Here's why:

- You can view driver ratings.
- You know they've had a background check.
- The booking is tracked from start to finish.

13. Accommodation

Knowing you are safe in your accommodation is crucial.

Research your accommodation thoroughly and remember that the requirements of a female solo traveller are different than that of say a family or a couple. Use sites like Booking.com, TripAdvisor, Airbnb and VRBO where you can check reviews from previous guests.

Avoid booking accommodation that doesn't have a review. Look for comments in relation to safety and specifically reviews from solo women. Booking.com allows you to filter by solo traveller, which is very useful.

If you feel unsure about anything, double and triple check. On a recent trip, I booked and paid for what I thought was an entire house to myself for a month through Airbnb. On arrival, I discovered that the owner's son was living in the house as the housekeeper and would be sleeping in the bedroom adjacent to mine. I immediately left, booked into a hotel and requested a refund from Airbnb on the premise that the advert was unclear. I have stayed in many Airbnbs, and this was certainly a first! It alerted me to the fact Airbnb descriptions are not always accurate and it's made me very cautious about booking accommodation for a whole month and paying upfront, without checking it out in person first. In this case, the host was new and didn't realise that he needed to advertise that it was a room in a shared property, but had I not been able to get a refund it would have ruined my holiday.

Check the location of the accommodation before booking to ensure that you will be in a safe neighbourhood. Again, what might be appropriate for a family might not be suitable for a solo woman. The idea of remote log cabin might sound lovely, but it's probably not the safest option on your own.

If you plan to go out at night, book a location you know is regarded as safe so that you don't need to worry about finding transport to get back. For instance, in Paris I'd feel perfectly safe in the Latin Quarter and could enjoy eating and exploring by foot in the evening, but I certainly wouldn't feel safe wandering about Gare de Nord after dark.

14. Ask your hotel staff

Hotel staff are not only there to check you in, but they are also usually locals who know the area well. Most staff are happy to help, so ask them about safe and unsafe places to go.

15. Alcohol

Enjoy a glass of wine in Paris, sip on an Aperol Spritz in Milan and a Margarita in Mexico but avoid getting sloshed at all costs. As a solo woman, you are much more of a target if you are drunk and it's really not worth the risk.

Generally, when I'm travelling alone, if I'm going to have alcohol it'll be one glass with a meal. If you plan to have a drink in a bar, ensure you order at the bar and never accept a drink from a stranger or someone you have just met. Drinks are easy to spike, and women alone are easy targets.

If you want to get sozzled, don't travel solo, go on a girlie holiday.

16. Evening activities

Evenings can seem like the trickiest part of the day as a female solo traveller. It can be difficult watching groups of friends or couples enjoying a meal and drinks together and you may feel unsafe wandering the streets by yourself.

However, it doesn't need to be difficult, you can turn the evenings into the time of day when you do a planned activity.

Check out Airbnb Experiences or Meetup for local evening activities. For example, you could go on a guided evening walk, attend a cookery class, enjoy local entertainment, or join an organised meal. They're a great way to fill your evenings with cool stuff and meet new people.

On a recent trip to Sri Lanka, I went to an organised cookery class with three other guests. It began at 4 pm with a tour around the market to buy produce for the meal, followed by 2 hours of cooking, followed by the delicious reward of all our hard work - eating! It was a fantastic way to share a meal, enjoy local food and learn some new cooking techniques. The transport home was arranged by the host, and I felt safe at all times.

17. Language

Okay, so you're probably not going to become fluent, but knowing a few basic words can go a long way. For example, words such as please, thank you and help are a few of the essentials, which are not only important in an emergency, but can also endear you to locals as they usually appreciate it if you make an effort with the language.

18. Learn basic self-defence

Knowing some basic defence moves will help you feel confident and prepared for your solo trip. I'd recommend something that is highly practical and applicable for everyday use such as Krav Maga.

19. Get a rape whistle

A rape whistle can be used in a range of situations including:

Personal attack – if someone tries to attack you, a rape whistle acts as a deterrent. One blast on the whistle will quickly alert others who are nearby and scare away your potential attacker.

Survival situations – if you are lost or injured in a natural environment, a whistle can alert someone that you need help. It could also be used to fend off wild animals.

Natural disasters – in the unfortunate event of natural disaster, a whistle can alert rescuers to your whereabouts.

Rape whistles are small enough to fit in your bag or to have on a keyring in your pocket. They are inexpensive and there are many on the market to choose from.

Other items that can be used in self-defence are keys and insect repellent.

Keeping Valuables Safe

20. Money

It sounds obvious but never flaunt large amounts of money.

Get a money belt or a crossbody bag. Avoid bags that you just hang from your shoulder, they are easy to swipe by someone nipping by on a scooter.

Don't have money in your pockets.

Don't carry more cash than you need. I tend to take out enough for a couple of days at the most.

Don't keep all your valuables in one place. Have cards or cash in different bags so that if you lose one, you know you have a back-up.

21. Passport

Print copies of your passport so you have a copy if it is lost or stolen.

Email yourself and loved ones an electronic copy of your passport so you know for certain you have a copy should you need it.

Some travellers like to keep their passports with them at all times, but I'm personally not keen. What happens if it is lost or stolen? Personally, I prefer to keep my passport locked up in my accommodation.

Admittedly, sometimes you'll need your passport. For example, if you plan to rent a car, visit certain tourist attractions and in some countries, you need your passport to pre-book trains. You can either take your passport with you on these occasions or alternatively, I have a photograph of my passport stored in my phone and this has sufficed to date.

22. Leave valuables at home

Leave any valuables at home, you don't need them whilst travelling and they can attract unwanted attention.

If you feel the need for jewellery, just keep it to dress jewellery, unless of course you're going up market and staying in a swish hotel and being driven to the opera.

23. Keep your mobile phone hidden

We're all very used to having our phones out, using Google maps to find a location, texting, chatting whilst we wander but remember, depending on where you are a decent smartphone could be a month's rent for some people in the world.

Don't make yourself a target. If you need to look at your phone, step inside a shop or café.

I sometimes use an old phone out in public and keep my expensive smartphone for indoors.

24. Get insurance

Don't skimp on travel insurance, it is simply not worth the risk! It can save you thousands if you need medical assistance or your personal property is stolen whilst you're away.

25. Scams

It's an unfortunate reality that tourists are easy targets in terms of being scammed so it's really useful to be aware of them so that you can try and avoid them. Research scams at your chosen destination before you go. There are many wild and ingenious ways scammers will try and get hold of your money, from women who try to give you a henna tattoo and then charge you before you've had time to think about what's going on to fake ATMs.

Here are some that I've experienced in my very recent travels – a broken taxi meter, a tuk tuk driver pretending not to understand my requested location and driving me miles out of the way and a tuk tuk driver claiming the hotel I booked was closed.

Wow a list of 25 safety tips – that sure makes the world seem like a dangerous place, doesn't it? And yet, truth be told, most female solo travellers including myself have not had a terrible experience whilst travelling. We've had fabulous experiences and met incredibly kind people who have gone out of their way to help us.

These tips are little helpers to ensure your risk remains low and to ensure you have a great time.

Chapter 9

COULD I COPE IN THE WORLD ALONE?

You are presented with two choices, evolve or repeat.

– Unknown

So, perhaps your partner is on-board, and you're over the moon excited but then there's this nagging voice inside your head that's freaking out at the thought of being alone on holiday; and why oh why did you think this was a good idea? You rationalise, you read numerous blogs, you checkout solo travel Facebook groups with seemingly squillions of other women who profess to love it, but secretly you wonder if you've really got the bottle.

'Jenny you've got balls' was what one friend said to me, when we were chatting about solo travel and writing this book. This made me laugh a lot and splutter out the coffee I was drinking. I could think of a number of retorts, but of course, I knew what she meant and that was – I'm not so sure I could travel solo because it's friggin' scary to be alone for so long.

I get it, I really do, but there's only one thing you can do if you feel this way.

Step right into the fear.

Life, as they say, does begin at the end of your comfort zone and that pesky fear that gets in the way is the hazy murky fog surrounding your comfort zone. It's the unknown, and woe and behold it stops you from seeing where you're going. How annoying! And yet when you step over that threshold of cosy comfort, into the fog of fear, do you know what happens? The fog magically lifts and, in its place, is a fresh azure sky, and there you are, basking, with vitality, nourishing your expanding soul.

You will cope.

You will probably thrive.

Just look at all the things you have done in life so far. I don't know your story, but perhaps it contains big things like study, a career, relationships, marriage, kids…and maybe some heartbreak and emotional upheavals. All these life events would have taken you beyond your level of comfort, even the exciting stuff – don't tell me that starting a new relationship or having a child isn't ever so slightly scary? And yet, with all these things, your heart and mind travelled, and you grew. You grew in ways you wouldn't have been able to imagine before doing them. The same will be true for solo travel.

There are many practical steps you can take so that you feel prepared both mentally and emotionally.

And remember, there's no rule that says you need to go for a long time when it's your first solo trip. Start off small, perhaps with a weekend break and see how you feel, and then build from this as your confidence grows.

In this section, we'll look at how to thrive when you're on your own.

I'm Freaking Out About Being Alone!

Solitude is the richness of the self.

– May Sarton

I often hear from friends that they love the idea of solo travel, or at the very least they're intrigued, but the fear of being alone stops them from taking the next step.

Worrying about being alone can usually be boiled down to these three reasons:

1. You're scared that you will be lonely.
2. You're freaked out by the idea of being 'seen' alone.
3. You're an extrovert and you simply love being around other people.

What's your reason?

1. You're scared that you will be lonely

Like all fears, the projection that you will be lonely comes from a place of not knowing. It's easy to concoct in your imagination that you'll be sat pining into a lonely cocktail as the days tick slowly by, but honestly on the contrary. As mentioned in Chapter 1, unless you specifically want to spend time alone it's relatively easy to meet people when travelling solo because you are naturally more open to other people, particularly other solo travellers. Thus, striking up a conversation and finding common ground is relatively straightforward.

If you're not convinced and the thought of spending long periods of time on your own gives you the collywobbles, but you still want to travel solo, see the **tips** below for ideas on how to meet people.

However, before you start booking yourself onto every social event going, take a step back and consider the positives of spending time alone. It's important to remember that being alone does not equate to loneliness, the two words are not interchangeable. Spending time alone offers you the invaluable opportunity to really enjoy your own company and get to know yourself. How many times in life do we really get the opportunity to just be by ourselves for a prolonged stretch of time?

Rather than worrying about being lonely, consider time spent alone as a gift to yourself.

Sure, there might be times when you will wonder why on earth you gave yourself so much quality 'me' time and feelings of unease may arise. But do you know what? That's okay. It's situations that challenge us emotionally and mentally, where our brains have to work a little harder and refigure a little that are really good for us. It's these situations that help us to grow.

Personal growth doesn't come from things that are easy and familiar. So, if you feel a little uncomfortable, welcome it. Say to yourself 'wahoo great, I'm going to sit with this feeling and let's see where it takes me…what can I learn?'

Maybe you'll learn that you hate solo travel. That too is great. You'll be able to sit firmly on the non-solo travel side of the fence knowing that you tried it and it wasn't for you.

Whenever you dip your toe into the cauldron of the unknown, you emerge having learnt something new about yourself and in all likelihood, you'll feel stronger for it.

2. Your're freaked out by the thought of being 'seen' alone

Are you cool with spending time alone, but the thought of others seeing you alone freaks you out? This is very common. We live in a society that for a long time has put socialising and the number of friends you have on a very high unrealistic pedestal, therefore worrying that you are being 'seen' as being alone is understandable.

It can feel like a totally irrational fear, because let's face it unless you're in your hometown no one will know who you are, and of course there's absolutely nothing wrong with being on your own, and yes, you're an adult! However, if you've ever had that sinking feeling of self-consciousness where you feel that everyone is looking and judging you for being sat alone – yes, the one that takes you straight back to the school playground, you'll know that it's not a nice feeling.

But here's the funny thing, researchers have done studies on the anxiety we feel in relation to how we think others perceive us when we are alone, and the truth of the matter is nobody cares what you're doing! Everyone else is too concerned with their own experiences and how they're coming across to be wondering why you're alone (Rosenbloom, 2019).

Furthermore, times are changing. As we discussed in Part 1, research shows that spending time alone has many benefits, and far from solitude being represented as something negative, people who choose to spend time alone are symbolic of people who are comfortable in their own skin.

I'd also like to point out that a confident woman sat alone, be it in a restaurant or on a sightseeing tour is sexy! I am not talking about trying to attract attention for being sexy (unless you want to, of course). I'm talking about inner sassy sexiness that makes you feel like a goddess – for you. The kind of self-assured sexiness that makes you feel in control and able to pursue your own dreams.

Lastly, although sat in your home before a solo trip, you may have visions of yourself being the only solo woman sat in a restaurant, let me quash those notions straightaway. Solo travellers are everywhere and there are some places where solo travellers seem to outnumber travellers with companions. I once entered a restaurant in Bali, and nearly every table was occupied by an unaccompanied woman. I promise you; you'll not be alone.

The best way to wipe out your fear of being seen to be alone, is 'fake it, until you make it.' Yep, pretend! When you pretend to feel confident, your brain literally learns how to feel confident – just like how it learns anything else. Our brains are made up of millions of neurons which communicate with each other via synaptic connections. The more we practice something the more hard wired those little connections become and learning takes place. We have the ability to create new connections all the time, therefore if you act 'as if' you are super laid back your brain will begin to learn that feeling and the more you do it, the more it becomes ingrained as a way of being. In no time, those feelings of unease will be banished.

How to practice looking and feeling confident alone:

- **Adjust your body language** – sit up, stand up straight and put your shoulders back. This immediately sends messages to your brain that you feel good.
- **Smile to yourself** – smiling causes pleasure chemicals such as dopamine, serotonin and endorphins to rush through your body thus increasing confidence levels.
- **Relax your face, jaw and body** – if you notice any tension then tell that part of the body to relax. I know that I tense my jaw and frown when I'm worried so I purposefully check those areas if I start to feel stressed and by noticing the tension, I can deliberately release it.
- **Breathe slowly and deeply from your diaphragm** – by practising nice slow breathing your body automatically begins to relax.

- **Wear something that makes you feel good** – you may not have a full wardrobe to choose from but even something as simple as a squirt of your favourite perfume can induce feelings of inner self-confidence.
- **Have something to do** – if you're sat at a café, a restaurant etc., having something to do whether it's a book, an iPad or your phone, always helps you feel more at ease and less conspicuous.

3. You're an extrovert and you simply love being around other people

If you fall into the extrovert camp, have no fear! You'll meet plenty of likeminded travellers on your trips.

See my **tips** below for meeting people when travelling solo.

Tried And Tested Ways of Meeting People When Travelling Solo

One of the benefits of solo travel is that you get to decide when you want to pop on your socialising hat, and when to hang it back up.

Here's a few tips on how to meet people:

Hostels – are great places to meet other travellers. Most hostels have lounges and kitchens, where you can relax, get on with some work, read or chat with other residents. If like me, you're fond of your own space, you don't need to stay in a dorm, most hostels these days offer single rooms, so you get the hostel communal living experience but with a little extra privacy.

Other accommodation – whether you stay in a homestay, a hotel or are renting a flat, your accommodation offers the perfect opportunity to meet and chat with people.

Tours & Airbnb experiences – there are a vast array of organised trips that you can join all over the world from wine tours in the Loire Valley, exploring the Masters in Florence to tea ceremonies in Japan and street food tours in Delhi. Just get yourself booked onto one and there you go - a readymade set of new people to chat away to.

Apps and social media – we don't have to rely on randomly meeting people these days (though of course this still happens!), there's a range of apps and solo travel Facebook groups to help us on our way (see Chapter 13, Useful Apps).

Yoga and other classes – I personally love yoga, and I find it a wonderful way to meet likeminded new people on a trip. There's nothing like a session of soothing asanas and then a good chat over coffee. Of course, if yoga isn't your thing, you could try any other type of class.

Volunteering – without a doubt volunteering is a wonderful way to meet fabulous people from all walks of life whilst putting back into the local community. My own experience of volunteering was immensely positive, I was welcomed warmly into the volunteer family, inspired by the kind hearts of the people I encountered and met lifelong friends.

Airports, trains, buses – believe it or not one of the easiest ways to spark up a conversation is whilst travelling. Standing around waiting for a delayed bus offers the perfect opportunity for chance friendships or at the very least a little company on the road.

Cafes – who doesn't love a coffee? There are now so many cool cafes where travellers, locals, and digital nomads hang out, particularly in cities. Start a casual conversation with someone on the next table and see where it takes you.

Language classes – I've not done this yet, but I really want to! There are language classes all over the world in fantastic locations. You can immerse yourself in your chosen language on a daily basis, stay with a local family to continue your practice and of course meet fellow students. I seriously need to learn Italian and I think this would be perfect!

Eating Alone

How do you feel about eating alone?

For many first-time solo adventuresses, the prospect of eating alone each day can be quite daunting, especially if it's not something you normally do.

I think most of us would agree that sharing a meal with others is one of life's pleasures, but that does not mean that eating alone cannot also be pleasurable, but in a different way.

Stephanie Rosenbloom describes the pleasure of eating alone perfectly in her book Alone Time. She suggests that 'We can breathe in and relish the flavours in a sauce, of the coolness of a pitcher of cream. We don't necessarily do these things in the presence of company, particularly during lively conversations. A solo meal is an opportunity to go slow; to savour' (2019, p.27).

Savouring our meals when we're alone takes practice. It's easy to gollop down our food without really tasting and enjoying it. It takes a conscious effort to slow yourself down and approach a meal as an experience to relish. In this way mealtimes become a memorable part of solo travel day.

I was fortunate in a previous job, that I was required to travel a lot throughout the UK and spend many nights in hotels, which of course meant lots of restaurant meals for one. It proved to be good practice for solo travel. Initially, I shied away from eating in fancy restaurants, they felt intimidating, and I felt self-conscious; but then one day peering and salivating at a menu, I concluded that by not eating in the nice restaurant I was limiting myself from having a new experience. So, I stepped inside and asked for a table for one.

I think on that first visit, I wolfed down my food and was out of there before you could say bon appetit, but that first time buoyed my confidence and from thereon after I went to whichever restaurant took my fancy.

I learnt to sit back, relax, order a 3-course meal with wine and savour it to the max. What was at first challenging, became something I grew to adore. I'd always have a book at the ready, in case I felt self-conscious, but more often than not I was quite happy to just soak in the atmosphere. If I began to feel paranoid that other diners were looking at me, I'd sit up straighter, smile to myself and curiously wonder if they felt a tad bit jealous that I was sat on my table for one. Or I'd imagine that I was the equivalent of Grace Dent (feisty British food critic) who I'm sure would roll her eyes at the mere thought of others judging her for eating alone.

It's all a matter of perception, change it and you'll feel like a million dollars.

It's also useful to note that eating alone is becoming significantly more common around the world. Busy lifestyles and the increased number of people living alone, has meant that eating alone has become a necessity and increasingly fashionable. Why? Because perceptions are changing – eating alone is no longer a sign that you're lonely, it's a sign you're confident and cool with your own company.

Where to eat

There's lots of choice when it comes to eating, here's a few ideas:

Restaurants

Fancy – just because you're alone you don't need to snack and dash. Don't shy away from ordering yourself a nice three course meal with a glass of wine in a fancy restaurant if that's what you desire. Learning to enjoy a meal by yourself is one of life's little pleasures.

Go casual – eating out doesn't have to mean a formal restaurant, you can take a casual approach, enjoy a magnifique pizza sat outside a pavement café in Rome as you watch the world unfold, who needs someone to chat to when you have the theatre of life playing out in front of you?

Eat your main meal at lunch time – if you feel self-conscious about eating alone consider making lunch time your main meal. It's much more common for people to eat alone in restaurants at lunchtime. Also, an added bonus of eating at lunch time is that menus tend to be cheaper than evening meals.

Informal Eating

If you don't fancy eating in a formal restaurant, there are lots of other options:

Street food – in many parts of the world street food is a way of life and part of everyday culture. It's a great way to enjoy the true authentic flavours of a place and learn about how local people eat. It also offers you the option of eating casually, whilst enjoying some amazing (some would say the best) food!

Markets & delis – fancy a picnic? Markets and delis are a great spot to pick up some delicious items for a picnic. French markets are one of my loves. Pick up a rotisserie chicken, some tomatoes, a baguette, some heavenly fresh quiches, followed by a petite cream cake and you have the perfect lunch.

Takeaways – don't fancy sitting in somewhere? Opt for a takeaway and eat in a park, by the river or wherever you fancy. Takeaways are by their nature casual and frequented by people on their own, so you definitely won't feel out of place. Furthermore, because of the pandemic, many takeaways and restaurants offer a home delivery service, so just like at home, if you don't feel like eating out, Uber Eats it!

Eating With Others

If you'd like a break from eating solo, there are plenty of ways that you can enjoy a meal with others. For example, check out Airbnb Experiences, you could join a cookery class and eat the meal afterwards, a street food tour – sample whilst you go, enjoy a meal in a local's house…the list is endless and it's a great way to try food with the people who know where to eat, as opposed to sticking to tourist joints. I've had some great foodie experiences in this way (see Chapter 13, Useful Apps).

PART 3

STORIES FROM
6 WOMEN IN RELATIONSHIPS WHO
TRAVEL SOLO

Part 3

STORIES FROM 6 WOMEN IN RELATIONSHIPS WHO TRAVEL SOLO

In the following pages six fabulous women in relationships tell you their stories of solo travel. They come from all walks of life and live across the globe, but what brings them together is their love of adventure and stepping out into the world alone. Their stories and insights reflect their passion for travel, the array of benefits, the challenges and the new doors that have opened.

FEATURING:

Katherine Leamy *The 5 Kilo Traveller*

Holly Worton *Author & Podcaster*

Sue-Anne Mayne *SisterStay*

Nicki Reilly *Online Business Coach*

Tegan Lewis *Heels to Heel Edge*

MaryJo Pham *The Silk Tea Co.*

Chapter 10

SIX WOMEN TELL THEIR STORIES

Katherine Leamy | The 5 Kilo Traveller

Starting out, I never meant to travel without my husband. It just happened. Thank God it did – it changed my life. Solo travel has been a game changer for me and everyone in my inner circle.

I'd originally planned to travel with a friend. We were well into the organisation of a girls' trip to Croatia and Italy from Australia and New Zealand, but her circumstances changed, and a four-week trip was no longer possible. I couldn't let the dream go. It wasn't the kind of trip my intrepid travelling husband would be into, with walks, cafes, pretty views, beaches. And with two teenage kids at home, I was looking for some me time! At the age of 47, who doesn't want a bit of that?

When I first broached the idea with him, he was hesitant and worried. I mean, he did do ALL our family's travel planning and was our built-in tour guide, driver, bag carrier and chief problem-solver. But that hadn't always been the case. I'd done a lot of intrepid travel in my 20s to South Africa, Zimbabwe, Namibia, Botswana, Egypt, Syria, Jordan, Israel, Turkey, Thailand, India and Nepal. I was an experienced traveller. I was more than capable, or so I tried to convince myself!

With a lot of planning and a carefully curated small day bag, weighing 13 pounds (5.5kg), I nervously boarded the plane to Dubrovnik. I was petrified.

Within a few days of arriving, my confidence grew. I was mesmerized by the scenery and history of the region. My fears of being mugged, murdered, ripped off, or losing my bag didn't happen. Instead, I was relishing this pure, blissful, *me time*. I could do as I wished, eat when I was hungry. I could eat dessert three times a day if I chose. I could sleep in or get up at 5am – usually the latter as I was often in my room by 8pm. I could change my plans on a whim. I only needed to consult myself, and I was usually agreeable to everything! I didn't have to go to any museums, unless bad weather forced me indoors.

I felt surprisingly safe and relaxed. I allowed plenty of time, so I was never rushing or making rash decisions.

The day I moved from Amalfi to Capri Island really summed up solo travel for me. I caught a ferry to the island. Unbeknown to me, I'd bought a daytrip ticket which included a tour of the entire, stunning coastline of Capri. It was fabulous. I could have been annoyed at my mistake, but this detour saved me a half-day island boat trip that I'd planned to do.

After getting off the boat I found huge queues for the funicular and the buses going up to the main town. Even though I was booked to stay two nights on the island, I didn't want to waste time in queues. With my small bag I was able to make the hour-long climb up the steps to the town of Anacapri where I was staying. There was no one else around. The views were jaw-dropping. The port and boats got tinier and tinier as I got higher and higher. I stopped when I felt like it and continued climbing once when I caught my breath. I set my own pace.

On reaching the top I sat with a cappuccino at a small café watching the tourists bustling by. I checked out a little garden grotto that looked out over the ocean towards Naples. I took the cable car up to the top of the mountain and chatted with locals. I sipped soda water at a café. I then went and explored the most artful home and enchanting garden of Axel Munthe.

I bought the most delicious potato and garlic pizza slices from a street vendor and walked back to the garden grotto overlooking the sea to eat them, alone. I wandered the labyrinth of streets to my hotel where I sat in my room on my shabby chic couch, watching the ocean below through the billowing net curtains. Stepping onto my balcony I pinched myself. Was I *really* here? I was surely in heaven.

I had 30 similar days like this. Sometimes I'd meet people on walking tours or daytrips, other days I spoke to shopkeepers, bakers, and bus drivers. I learned to be content eating alone and realized that no one cared or noticed I was at a table for one. I wore the same outfits, and no one noticed. People were open to talking to a solo female traveller. I posed no threat. On the road I wasn't just Katherine, the mum or the nurse. I was a fellow traveller. I was greeted by people younger and older than me. I was just me and I felt very accepted.

I found time passed slowly. Halfway through my trip I felt like I'd been away for two months rather than two weeks. I was acutely aware of what was going on around me. Afterall, there was only me to keep myself safe. I stayed centrally. I didn't do things I wouldn't do at home. I was careful, aware, and vigilant. My confidence and bravery soared.

Solo travel was a reboot for me. I found a bit of my old self, and relied a lot on my new wiser self. Feeling more confident has enriched my relationships with my husband and kids. I'm surer of my decisions and what I want to do. I'm in charge of my own life. I steer my own ship. I learned to trust my gut instinct and have the confidence that I can rise to a lot of challenges. I'm a lot stronger and braver than I ever believed.

Solo travel in a relationship. My husband didn't initially understand why I wanted to travel solo. After the trip I explained the benefits of spending some time on my own. It's not his preferred travel style, but he definitely saw the positive change in me. I gained more confidence to stand up for what I wanted in our relationship and in my life.

I don't think you can do something like this and not change. The important thing is to keep talking with your partner. Explain why you need this, and that it's not about rejection or turning away. We all need space to grow. It also helped me give him space for the things that he wants to do for himself.

Solo travel is now an accepted and expected part of my self-care strategy. I've since travelled solo to China, Australia and around New Zealand, and have so many more wonderful solo adventures planned.

If you're keen to give solo travel a go, here are my top tips:

1. Travel light – it makes getting around a lot easier.
2. Practice with an overnight before you go on a big trip – try a weekend away by yourself to somewhere you are familiar with.
3. Follow the same safety rules you have at home – don't wander unknown neighbourhoods, avoid poorly lit areas, drink safely or go out with others and stick together, let people know where you are.
4. Reach out to other solo travellers for support and ideas. There are a lot of us out there.

At the end of the day, we only have one life. This is no dress rehearsal.

Learn more about Katherine:
www.the5kilotraveller.com
Instagram @the5kilotraveller
Facebook www.facebook.com/the5kilotraveller

Holly Worton | Author & Podcaster

My solo travel adventures started when I was single, back in the mid-90s when I was studying abroad in Spain. After a fun but slightly stressful trip with two of my housemates, I decided to take my next trip on my own. I loved it: I could do what I wanted, when I wanted, however I wanted. It was travel bliss.

I continued to travel solo for years until I ended up in a particularly stifling long-term relationship where it was clear that solo travel was not an option for me. We were business partners as well and I felt like we were joined at the hip – not in a good way. The relationship lasted for about a decade, and by the time it was over I had forgotten the joy of solo travel.

In 2009 I began a new relationship with the man who is now my husband. My lifestyle now is the polar opposite of how it was during my previous relationship. Where before there was restriction, now there is freedom.

My first solo trip was to Italy, at that time we had been together for just one year. Because of my background, I was nervous about heading overseas for the ten-day trip. I was heading to the annual gathering of friends from our spiritual group, and I would be surrounded by people I knew – but I would be travelling alone.

I kept checking in every few hours, feeling guilty if I didn't provide my partner with a regular update. It felt unbelievable that I had the freedom to travel on my own. It felt like I was doing something wrong, something naughty. But it was the shift back into solo travelling that I needed.

Later that year we moved to England, and a few years after we settled in I embarked on regular solo travel: I walked the South Downs Way, the Ridgeway National Trail, the Downs Link and the

Wey-South Path. I started camping on my own, heading down to a beautiful campground just an hour from home, where I would run the trails, read a book by the campfire and relax.

It was about that time that I also started my monthly workcations. Workcation weekends are the laser-focused getaways that I use to work on creative projects, like books or other writing projects. They're so satisfying and so powerful that I've written a book on the topic, to encourage others to give them a try.

I also take solo trips for various outdoor courses that I've done over the years: ethnobotany, wildlife trailing and plant identification. Many of these involve camping at the site, so I'm away for a long weekend or even a week. These are all topics that my husband isn't interested in, so it makes sense for me to go alone.

But I'm not the only one who travels solo – my husband also goes on occasional workcations, and when he returns home to visit Argentina he travels on his own. He also travels to continental Europe for long weekend trips with his spiritual group.

My husband and I both work from home, and we have done so for over a decade. Because we spend so much time together in a very small house, our solo trips give us the time and space to do our own thing on our own terms.

When I asked my husband how he felt about my solo travel, he said this: "I feel great about it. I think that we all need to have our own space to explore and expand our horizons, especially through travelling and all things related to hiking and running. It's never been challenging, except for usual concerns about safety, lack of phone coverage, etc. Benefits: the best one is, it allows us both to bring more to the table for our relationship."

My top tip for anyone who is in a relationship but wants to travel solo is this: communicate. Make sure your partner knows how important solo travel is to you. Ask your partner how they feel about your solo travel.

Create a plan for keeping in touch: will you text? Phone? Share photos of what you're doing? Get clear on exactly what would help them to feel comfortable about your solo trip.

Just as important: start small. Go on a weekend getaway. Then go away for a week. Then stretch it to something longer. And communicate, communicate, communicate.

Solo travel is now a deal-breaker for me in a relationship. I clearly understand how unhealthy my previous relationship was, where I felt cut off from my beloved solo travel. And I never again want to feel restricted in that way. Freedom is one of my highest values, and I will continue to seek it out through healthy life choices.

Happy solo travels!

Learn more about Holly:
www.hollyworton.com
Instagram @hollyworton
Facebook www.facebook.com/HollyWortonPage

Sue-Anne Mayne | SisterStay

I think I first caught the travel bug as a 17-year-old, straight out of high school on an exchange year to Japan. Everything about my new life as the only "gaijin" in a town of some 35,000 people in northern Japan was so far removed from my everyday upbringing in Australia, it ignited in me a sense of adventure and curiosity that has been with me ever since.

I spent many subsequent years to-ing and fro-ing between Japan and Australia – and other countries – before ultimately marrying an Englishman and moving to the UK. At first we did quite a bit of travel together, but over the years, especially whilst bringing up three young children, we got into the habit of mostly me travelling on my own and primarily to Australia to catch up with family and friends. It was simply too expensive for us all to go on a regular basis, so it made sense for me to go by myself.

As much as I missed my family in the UK – and I really did miss them – I felt an enormous sense of freedom and excitement pretty much as soon as I stepped onto that plane. My senses suddenly became extra heightened to new ideas and experiences, and I rediscovered some of the previously boundless creativity I had unwittingly stifled in order to give my all to my family. I found myself making copious notes about interesting avenues to pursue and topics to look up when I got home. I would draft outlines for novels. (No, I'm not a writer but I always feel inspired to write when I am travelling!) I would strike up conversations with random strangers discussing all kinds of weird and wonderful subjects. It was liberating and rejuvenating and made me a much happier person to live with.

Meanwhile, my husband, who was brought up in the country, had settled into contented midlife. His favourite places to go are the ones our loyal dog can go too, and he revels in the simple pleasures of having our geese nibble his wellie boots while he potters in the garden.

Whilst I appreciate the little pleasures too, it's not enough for me. The 'me' that thrives on adventure loves to venture further. Exploring new places and meeting new people, stepping out of my ordinary life and into an alternative one, just for a few days or weeks at a time, enables me to recharge my batteries. Quite often I will combine it with taking a short course in something or visiting a far-flung exhibition which is only on for a limited period. It's such fun to inject that element of adventure into my otherwise pedestrian existence.

Planning where to stay on these little forays, however, has not always been my favourite thing to do. I'm not into dossing in cheap hostels and I couldn't afford to stay in swanky boutique hotels. Finding safe and affordable accommodation was always a challenge. Yet I suspected there were loads of older women like me who would love to spread their wings if it were just a little bit easier to do so.

I tried zooming in on the faces of Airbnb hosts to see who they were, although it's becoming increasingly difficult to find affordable rooms in the homes of ordinary people amongst the sea of SuperHosts. I spent hours scrolling through the comments on solo travel articles looking for hints as to where people were staying. I Googled "women only accommodation" and "safe travel for older women" and trawled through several couch-surfing style websites, but eventually, I just decided to take the plunge and set up my own homestay community.

After years of staying with friends and family in Australia, I realised I just needed a comfortable bed in a warm and friendly home, preferably with another woman as my host. I didn't require someone to look after me at all or do too much handholding, but I did want that sense of coming "home" at the end of each day. Perhaps to a glass of wine and a catch-up chat. To hear from a local where were the best places to visit or even to avoid. To know, if worse came to worst, I had a friend nearby who I could call on. I wanted to be able to travel independently, but safely, giving peace of mind to both me and my husband.

And so SisterStay was born. "A welcome home wherever you travel." Ordinary women – the majority single, but some married, like me - opening their homes to one another to make this next chapter one to really remember.

Every new member is personally ID-verified and keen to make the most of life. It might be she offers a single room with a shared bathroom. Or a king-sized room with its own en-suite. But we don't care which because we are all part of the same community, charging the same overnight fee - which is just enough to cover costs and provide a little bit of pocket money. And we're all glowing in the knowledge that we are helping each other to live our very best, most adventurous lives, with or without a partner at home.

Learn more about Sue-Anne:
www.sisterstay.com
Instagram @sister_stay
Facebook www.facebook.com/SisterStay

Nicki Reilly | Online Business Coach

My husband and I met through travel. But not in the way you would expect from that statement. We both, independently, lived and worked at summer camps in the US and travelled across the country afterwards, each for 5 years, always in different places, always completely unaware of each other's existence.

Following these independent experiences, we both found ourselves living and working in London, as young 20-somethings, for the company that had helped make these experiences possible. This is where we met, living, and working in London. We had a shared love of travel, and I knew for certain that I was nowhere near done exploring this world, not even close.

There's an expectation when you're in a committed relationship that all of your future travel experiences will be together. While there's of course a lot to be enjoyed about sharing experiences with your loved one, this doesn't need to mark the end of your solo adventures. I love my husband, of course, and we've had some truly incredible adventures together and I look forward to many more.

However, I personally believe that we, as in the grander meaning of that word, collectively, could vastly benefit from having more focus on being whole, independent, happy humans first and to bring these full selves to a relationship, rather than losing a sense of identity or independence as many can in becoming a pair. Rather than the alternative -- looking for that other person to complete us in a sense or even as a definition of happiness or success in today's society.

A few years into our relationship, my work situation allowed for me to spend another summer living, working & adventuring in the states, his did not. Not only that, but these experiences were ones I actually preferred to have alone. It absolutely would have been easy at that moment to dismiss the notion and simply spend the time together in London instead. Many would and did argue that this would have been the easier option entirely and I completely understand that point of view. But here's the thing I've come to know, and I'm proud to say that I've kept it as a basis to many of my decisions:

A comfort zone is a beautiful place, but nothing ever grows there.

So what did we do? We made the simultaneously uncomfortable & exhilarating decision to spend the summer apart.

There are notions we have in life - soul nudging type feelings and they don't come by accident. This was one of those moments. I'm willing to wager that many of us ignore hundreds of these moments in our lifetime. But here's the thing - our existence here is an absolute miracle. The chances of our existence on this mass orbiting around the universe at the speed of light are approximately 4 trillion to one. Let that sink in for a second. We are all individuals whose existence here is nothing short of miraculous. We are unique and we have different desires and different things that set our souls on fire. While my personal relationship was founded through travel, travel continues to provide more of an ongoing pull to me than it does my husband. Plus, there's a truly different experience to be had when experiencing something solely through your own lens than through a shared one.

For many like-minded souls, this will intrinsically make sense, as though it's a part of who you are. To others, it will be a challenging concept that makes you feel uneasy. Both perspectives are completely valid, and I have resonated with both at different points in my life experience so far. Even as a born dreamer and wanderer, everything is like a muscle and when you don't use it, you can lose it. Taking the leap back into the world of solo travel after not exercising that muscle for some time, can feel uncomfortable. The thing is - when we're not challenging ourselves, we aren't growing, something I truly believe this human experience is about, always growing.

Traveling alone will likely be the scariest, most liberating, life-changing experience of your life. So please, try it at least once.

My love for travel and curiosity about the world led me to the work that I now do online. The freedom to work from anywhere makes my wandering soul smile. Life is too short to be lived in one place.

I write this from my balcony listening to the ocean on a solo night away and I'm reminded of the power of the space provided by experiencing somewhere new, alone. Connection to self, peace, confidence, personal growth and appreciation for my life with my husband are just some of the positives that come to mind. Never lose sight of who you are as an individual. My wish for the world is that no one ever misses out on a life experience by giving weight to the flawed logic: 'I don't have anyone to go with.' Always, follow those soul nudges to wander.

This world is wide, real & waiting for you.

Learn more about Nicki:
https://bio.site/nickireilly
Instagram: @nickireilly__

Tegan Lewis | Heels to Heel Edge

The thought of travelling solo had never really crossed my mind.

I had travelled the world with my husband and was in love with the idea of travel generally, but I had never really considered travelling without him. It wasn't until he got a job where he had to travel the world, and because of our situation back home in New Zealand I could only join him for parts of it, that I was essentially forced by circumstance to take my first solo flight to meet up with him.

But those five long flights from Auckland to Alicante needed some kind of circuit breaker, and so I arranged a stop-over in Dubai. And something stirred in me on that brief stop in a new country on my own for the first time – a sense of adventure and freedom that I had not previously experienced when travelling before.

I of course missed my husband though and couldn't wait to see him, and I enjoyed every moment in Alicante that we got to spend together outside of him working. Although that free time was fleeting, and I soon became restless – I was keen to return to Barcelona; a place nearby that I had visited before with him and fallen in love with. He was unable to take the time off work and so I thought, heck, why not just go myself?

And so I did, armed with a newfound confidence, and the realisation that I didn't have to wait for the stars to align for other people to join me in order to make trips happen.

A number of years passed, and I did not manage to take another truly solo trip, but we had travelled to many countries and even lived in San Francisco and then Italy, and so I had explored many new places on my own at times.

Then one day the rug was pulled out from under me, and I was suddenly alone; my marriage was over. At the time we were visiting in New Zealand but still lived in Italy – so I had no job, no home, no car, and everything I owned was either in Italy or a storage container.

Everyone of course thought it was best that I stayed in New Zealand surrounded by people who loved me and would support me, but something within me told me otherwise.

I don't know how to explain it, but I knew I needed to be on my own. It sounded crazy to everyone, even to me, but something in my intuition told me that time by myself was what I needed to heal.

So I spent around three months travelling solo around Europe – meeting up with old friends, making new ones, and just generally truly indulging in my own company for the first time in years.

On that journey I found many things – I found that I was capable of more than I thought I was, both emotionally and physically, and that I was often more comfortable being on my own than I was with others. I found that I had spent so many years thinking about and trying to please someone else that I had truly forgotten who 'I' was – and this time travelling alone pushed me to find that person again. With every step I took I awoke another part of me that had laid dormant for years; with every new person I met, I met a new part of myself as well.

But solo travel when you're single or when circumstances dictate is one thing – solo travel by choice in the context of a relationship can present entirely different challenges.

Many years, trips and moves later, I met my current partner while we were both working a ski season in the French Alps, and after the season ended we decided to move to London together.

We both came into the relationship with totally different angles on travel – I was obviously ready to get right into it, wanting to get away and see and do as much as possible, especially while living in London, and was happy to travel with my partner, friends, or alone.

My partner on the other hand was more of a 'you travel to relax, in one place, for a defined period' type. He had grown up with Europe on his doorstep and so the 'easy' travel afforded by being based in London was not a novel concept to him as it was to me, plus he was a chef and so had basically no free time, and what little time he did have he (understandably) just wanted to relax at home.

We spent some time unconsciously trying to sway the other towards our own way of thinking – me encouraging him to join me on trips hoping he would catch the travel bug and love it too, and him coaxing me into time spent doing as little as possible.

Over time we communicated (albeit not always constructively!) and worked out what each other's boundaries were, and what our concerns, needs and desires were. It wasn't always easy – and still isn't – but we work towards understanding, accepting and appreciating our differences, and how we accommodate them in our relationship.

I established that travel was not only a chapter of my story, but rather that it is part of my identity. It is how I light a fire in my soul, where I derive my creativity and joie de vivre from, where I find my confidence and my passion. And my partner established that he enjoys going slowly in his free time, that he takes pleasure and regains strength in time spent fishing and diving or doing very little.

Over the years things have changed a lot – we now live in New Zealand, my partner is no longer a chef, we have a house and pets and other responsibilities and focusses. As a result, the ways in which we value spending our time are now more aligned than ever before. However, we of course still have our differences, and continue to try to give each other the space and time to fill our respective cups.

For anyone considering whether solo travel within the context of a relationship is possible – it absolutely is. But as with literally anything in a relationship – you need at the very least, communication, respect and compromise.

Communicate: tell the other person why you want to travel solo and why it is important to you, find out what concerns they might have with you travelling solo and talk about how you might work together to mitigate those concerns.

Respect: hear what the other person is saying and empathise with their words – don't simply jump on the defensive or offensive. Try to understand where they are coming from and again work together not against one another.

Compromise: it might be that no compromise is needed, but it is often the case if two people are coming at something from different directions. Always be willing to find out where the middle ground lies, so you can work together to get to that point.

Even if you and your partner both share a love of travel, there is still nothing to preclude you from being able to travel solo – a relationship is a mutual partnership, not a tether to another person.

So, if you're considering travelling solo then simply open a dialogue with your partner about it, and then hopefully in no time you'll be enjoying an adventure that you can't wait to tell them all about.

Learn more about Tegan:
Instagram @heelstoheeledge
Instagram @outdoorbathsnz
www.heelstoheeledge.com
Facebook www.Facebook.com/groups/shespreadherwings
Facebook www.Facebook.com/groups/SFHR.NewZ

MJ Pham | The Silk Tea Co.

An Interview

Can you describe some occasions when you have travelled solo?

I used to think that travel was only meant to coincide with local public holidays or special occasions. When I was older — by the time I had lived abroad in several countries alone — I realized that travel itself can be a special occasion. Life is a special occasion, and we have an unknown quantity of time here. As a woman, solo travel can be an extraordinarily empowering experience — one that can connect us to our senses and energize us with wonder, gratitude, and joy.

Some of my most precious memories are from my solo trips, including my time in Argentina, Cambodia, the Dominican Republic, Italy, France, Malaysia, Mexico, Morocco, Norway, the Philippines, Poland, Portugal, Spain, the United Arab Emirates, and Vietnam. Each trip has contributed to my memory bank of scents, sights, sounds, flavours, and emotions …

On one of my trips in 2017, I remember an unforgettable rainbow stretching across the sky, over the tops of the swaying palm trees. It was a sight to behold after being soaked while driving alone through an afternoon downpour, navigating potholes on my rented motorbike on the island of Siargao in the Philippines.

Another memory I have still lingers on the tongue. I can still taste the cardamom and rich creaminess of camel milk in the *karak chai* that was served on one of my trips to the Emirates, when I sat with a wonderful blanket of stars above me in the desert. It reminded me of the incredible friendships I made with women like myself in nearby Saudi Arabia, where I once lived and worked.

And once, when I couldn't get my cellphone to work at the airport in Krakow, Poland, a kind young woman helped me acquire a SIM card and set up my phone. Anastasiya and I became friends as we later met up in the town for coffee and a tour, and we have kept in touch as friends across the miles ever since, updating each other on our careers, the state of our hearts, and our dreams. So even though I may travel solo, I know I don't have to be in solitude — I'm never alone, unless that's a choice I make.

What prompted these solo ventures?

An intrinsic curiosity about how life is lived elsewhere, and a desire to taste it. In each new place I venture, I always ask myself, *Could I live here? What would it feel like, look like, and taste like?* And I set off to have that experience. This has taken me to gorgeous vineyards in Mendoza, Argentina and to unforgettable walks along the Atlantic coast in the town of Matosinhos, Portugal.

I have been traveling solo for a long time. If one is just starting out, I recommend starting right in town, where you are. How would you spend the day as a visitor, what treasures would you seek to find? And then let your love of traveling evolve from there. For me, once I moved to Singapore in 2016 and to New York City in 2018, I was always on the lookout for airfare deals to far-flung locales. Airline loyalty programs and sites such as Google Flights and Scott's Cheap Flights really helped me identify fabulous deals and galvanized me to get going! I have found roundtrip airfare to Europe from the United States for less than $300. It is hard to turn a deal like that down.

Can you describe how you feel when you travel alone?

It's such a joy — I like to think of all the positive possibilities, the opportunity for discovery, self-reflection, and rest, for example.

One of my favourite sayings is, "When nothing is sure, anything is possible." With each trip, I ask myself, *How do I want to live on this trip?* Sometimes, I want to travel as a teamaker, to gather inspiration for new tea blends — so that involves a lot of tasting, eating, and drinking. Sometimes, I travel as a scuba diver to honour my love of marine life. That involves pre-booking certifications and excursions. And sometimes, all I am seeking is bone-deep rest, solo. So that can mean time by the sea, or time spent getting massages. And there are travel arrangements available for every budget.

I always feel excited about possibilities of what *can go right*. Who I might meet or befriend by chance, the meals I might stumble across or plan to reserve months in advance ... for me, a lot of the joy is doing research beforehand to bookmark a few places I want to see or experience, while leaving blocks of time for wandering and organic discovery once I am there.

I find that *planning* some parts of my solo trip allows me to have an easy time on the ground once I am there. I like to pick up magazines or guidebooks, and I love searching online for places where I can enjoy local delicacies, book a shopping trip, or attend a fitness or dance class (I took a belly dancing class in Norway)!

How do you benefit from solo trips?

Each trip is a chance to build more trust with myself. It is a bridge to getting to know myself better. I don't have to spend my vacation or trip worrying about if a tripmate is happy, satisfied, if they're bored by my window shopping... or annoyed that I want to stay in the museum for longer. Instead, solo travel is the art of being self-aware. Each destination has revealed my strengths, and also my weaknesses — aspects of myself I can improve. I learned that I take joy in planning and can also welcome spontaneity. I also know I can be more patient and take time to savour things more slowly.

With each trip, I always marvel at how much there is to learn from others who live their own lives elsewhere, with different languages, faiths, beliefs woven across the fabric of their society. While some trips have had low moments — getting lost, having a car rental breakdown, being afraid of crime — I will say I also am in awe of the luck I have had in meeting kind strangers. Standing in queues or long lines have sparked lovely conversations, spontaneous friendships, that sort of thing. Choosing different excursions and experiences have led to memorable dinners with fascinating people who are also traveling solo, or couples and families curious about how and why I choose to travel alone. As hard as this world can be, there is also much to appreciate in the kindness and beauty of some strangers we can meet along our journey, especially when we travel new to spaces, be they small hamlets, cities, or entire countries.

I will never forget my first solo trip to Italy. I decided to make a long weekend of it and travelled to Rome in December 2019, one of the last trips I took before the pandemic. This solo sojourn was one that truly changed my life — connecting me to a language and culture I love, helping me understand the cuisine and viticulture, allowing me to celebrate my body confidence by exploring Italian fashion, and ultimately, this trip introduced me to the man that would become my husband.

Do you think there are any benefits to your relationship during your time apart?

Absolutely! I say this having the deepest love and utmost care for my partner, my family, and friends: The most important relationship I will ever have is the one I have with myself. I love the opportunity of getting to *miss* my partner and my routines, and the sense of gratitude each time I feel when I return *home*. I also like to pretend I am a travel writer sometimes, and on trips, I will take notes for friends and bookmark places where I would one day love to return with my partner or loved ones.

Have you encountered any challenges when travelling solo?

To travel is to understand that not *everything* will go according to plan, and to know that *this* is part of the magic. Trips will not unfold like they flawlessly do on social media, and yet, we travel anyway — because for the most part, the rewards are greater than the challenges we might encounter along the way.

I think it is so important to have a romantic relationship that respects the healthy rituals you have for yourself. It can be difficult to say goodbye to our loved ones when we travel, but it is an investment of time and money that allows us to reset and refresh ourselves. And with today's technology, we can always check in with our people on video calls and share our locations in real-time if we need to, so they know we are safe.

Now, all travellers, especially those of us who identify as women, can be vulnerable in new cities or countries. Take care to read the news for the latest insights into where you are going, purchase medical and travel insurance that meets your needs, register with your embassy in the locality where you are visiting, and be sure your emergency contacts know of your itinerary and whereabouts. Plan to have regular check-in times so your loved ones know you are safe. If you are traveling somewhere, you have never been, I recommend you share your location on Google Maps with a trusted contact, for example, so they can look after you from afar. Look for female travel guides and women-owned businesses for excursions and activities once you are on the ground, they are often more than happy to support you in the sisterhood of solo travel.

Do you have any tips for women who are thinking about travelling solo, but are hesitant because they're in a relationship?

Your most important relationship is the one you have with yourself. Approach your trips with a plan to honour the light within yourself — get to know how you can meet your own desires, wants, dreams, and needs. Always dreamed of seeing a Broadway show in New York City? Take yourself! Curious about running or cycling in a race abroad? Register and go! Hungry to learn how to make the best Thai dishes or to taste Haitian coffee at its source? Book a trip for yourself. Absolutely dying to visit the Amalfi Coast? Book the trip and go, *bella!* Solo travel is the best gift you can give yourself. It is a gift of time and perspective.

Note: these views are mine and don't represent any other organisation or affiliation.

Learn more about MJ:
www.thesilktea.co
Instagram @thesilkteaco

Chapter 11

TOGETHER, BUT APART

Tips for Maintaining a Strong Bond Whilst You're Away

It's time to do the happy dance, yeah baby!!! You are going to travel solo.

I'm so excited for you.

The tips below offer a few suggestions that you may want to consider for maintaining a healthy bond during your time apart. No doubt, you'll think some are a good idea and others not. Pick what you fancy, dabble, play – it's all about feeling comfortable with the new shared chapter you're about to begin.

Pre-Trip Tips

Communication Strategy – have you discussed and come up with your communication strategy? (See Chapter 7). Remember communication is the crux of a successful period apart. Get into the habit of talking openly about your feelings to stop them from festering.

Boundaries – have you come up with some ground rules for safety and trust? Have you set a date to review and check in on those ground rules? (If not see Chapter 7 & 8).

Plan together – some couples find it useful to do some of the planning for the trip together. This creates a feeling of it being a shared experience and helps to reduce the unknown and alleviate safety concerns.

Plan something special before you go – it doesn't need to be extravagant, but it's nice to do something to celebrate your love and gratitude towards each other. Perhaps this has been quite a difficult journey for you and perhaps you've had some challenges along the way, so celebrate how far you've come. Crack open a bottle of bubbly. Make a toast to your bravery, solidarity and love, to living life on your terms and to making your relationship your own.

During Your Trip

Spending time apart doesn't mean that you have to stop doing things together. There are plenty of ways to enjoy each other's company even when you're miles apart.

Plan remote dates – here's an opportunity to use your imagination and think of all the ways you could have a remote date with your loved one. What do you both love doing? Do you like watching films together, or have a favourite Netflix series? Well, why not arrange a date and watch something together. Both Netflix and Amazon Prime have watch party options. Or perhaps, listening to podcasts or online games is your shared thing.

Share songs – we all have songs that touch us deeply and we often have songs that hold meaning for us as a couple. Playing each other your favourite songs is a beautiful way to connect digitally. Spotify is a nice way to share songs. Why not create a romantic playlist?

Plan some intimate time – dim the lights, play your favourite music and indulge in a little sexy time. Sexual desire is not only about connecting physically but also emotional connection. If sharing your intimacy digitally is new to you, it may feel weird and it's normal to feel a little shy. Talk about how you feel and discuss your boundaries. One of the beauties of sharing awkward feelings is it's often a step towards a place of deeper intimacy.

Read the same book – have you heard the saying 'couples who read together stay together?' Reading or listening to audio books is a lovely way to share whilst apart and also makes for an interesting discussion after you've listened/read a chapter. Novels are an excellent choice, but equally, you could choose a book that provokes reflection and deeper discussion. For example, this might be a perfect opportunity to read/listen to a book on mindfulness or self-development. You can then discuss the pertinent points after a chapter.

Share poetry – poetry is a lovely way to share your heartfelt emotions. Poems tap into the soul, and nothing beats a poem to say exactly how you feel. You could look up a poem or even better you could both write one and send it.

Share photos – I always think there's a fine line with sending photos, I don't like to barrage my loved one with tonnes of photos, but I do like to give him a feel of what I'm up to. Therefore, I select photos carefully and include a description. That way, I'm not just sharing a pretty picture but a snapshot of my day.

Be spontaneous – we've talked a lot about planning, but don't forget to be spontaneous. A spontaneous 'I love you' can make someone's day.

Start a blog – blogs are easy to set up and they can be a great way to share your journey with your partner, friends and family.

Post-Trip

I'll leave this one to you, it's time to celebrate…

Chapter 12

PRACTICAL TIPS FOR GOING SOLO

Wahoo, you're going to travel solo! You've made the decision and you're raring to go!

Once that decision is made, it's time to get practical and start figuring out how you're going to make that dream into a reality.

This section covers:

- Picking your location
- Deciding on your holiday type
- Choosing your accommodation
- Useful tips

Let's go!

Picking Your Location

So where are you going?

Choosing your destination has to be the most exciting part of planning any trip, right?

The choices, the choices…

Maybe you already have a destination you're desperate to go to, or maybe you're overwhelmed by the sheer choice of so many delicious destinations! Wherever you decide, I'm sure it will be amazing.

However, if you're struggling to decide on a location, it's completely understandable because planning a solo trip isn't quite as straightforward as sticking the pin in a map.

Here's a few tips to get you started:

Start Small

If you feel apprehensive, start small. You don't need to fly halfway across the world to travel solo. You could stay in your home country and take a city break or simply go away for one night. By starting small, you can build your confidence before going further afield and figure out if solo travel is right for you.

Take a leaf of Nicki's book (see Part 3), she relishes the opportunity for a single night away to reconnect with herself and reflect; or do as MaryJo suggests and start in your own town – pretend you're a visitor and see what treasures you can find.

I personally love a solo trip to London every now and then. It's only a two-hour train trip for me and it's just the ticket to get my solo juices flowing before embarking on a bigger trip.

Pick Your Location Wisely

Choosing the right destination for your first solo trip is important. You want to feel comfortable, and you don't want to have too many unnecessary worries.

Here are a few things to consider:

- How far do you want to travel?
- Do you want to go somewhere with a familiar culture and language?
- Is it popular with other female solo travellers?

There are ample resources on the internet for solo female travellers and lots of valuable insight into good locations for solo women. Of course, this is highly subjective, and what is right for one person is not necessarily right for another. However, if lots of female travellers are saying they didn't like a location, then I'd probably avoid it for a first trip. For example, I was recently contemplating a trip to Morocco, but as I reflected on a previous trip to Marrakesh with a friend, I remembered that we experienced a lot of male hassling. I decided to check out what other solo women said about Morocco and unfortunately the overwhelming majority stated that they wouldn't go back as they felt unsafe.

I therefore decided against Morocco as my first trip following a two-year break from solo travel due to the pandemic. That's not to say, I wouldn't go – I'd still love to visit – but it was important to me on that first post pandemic trip that I felt comfortable, safe and secure.

If you were to really push me (really push) to pinpoint just 3 locations that I would say yes, they are super for first time female solo travellers, I'd say:

1. Bali – it's a mecca for us solo ladies thanks to the memoir Eat, Pray, Love and you'll certainly never feel out of place as a solo woman, in fact you'll feel very much in the majority.
2. Slovenia – I felt very safe in this tiny country. It's ranked as one of the safest and greenest countries in the world. It's beautiful, eclectic, and very female friendly.
3. Italy – yep, us ladies have been solo tripping to Italy for a long time, so again you won't feel out of place and of course it's got the whole Italian thing going on. Check out the stories in Part 3, it's no coincidence that myself, Katherine, and Holly all chose Italy as our first solo trip!

Go Somewhere You've Been Before

Who says you need to go someone new on your first solo trip? No one. If you've been somewhere in the past and you like the idea of returning by yourself then this is an excellent option for a first trip. You'll already have an idea of what to expect, thus taking away an element of the unknown and the experience you'll have solo will be very different than any previous trips.

Type of Travel

The next step is to decide on the type of travel you want to do; just because you're travelling solo doesn't mean that you need to do it totally alone, there are many options available from organised holidays to retreats.

Here are a few ideas:

Organised Solo Holidays

Due to increased demand, the number of tour companies offering organised holidays for solo travellers has skyrocketed in recent years. Canadian-based travel agency G Adventures stated, 'solo travellers made up 51% of it's bookings this year – and 70% of them are female, up slightly from 2019' (Ng, 2022). This has resulted in some travel firms wavering single room supplements and increasing the number of single rooms.

Many companies offer exciting immersive experiences, often with the guarantee of sustainability. This could be a great way forward if you want to travel solo, but don't want the stress of doing it all by yourself and like the idea of having people to share the experience with.

I've not been on an organised trip, so I can't offer any personal insights but from what I've read it seems that all you need to do is pick the location, the type of holiday you want, pay and the company does the rest. Easy, just turn up and go. On the negative side, they tend to be quite pricey, and schedules can be tight, so if you don't like being shuttled from one activity to another this may not be for you.

Check out:
Intrepid – has over 30 years' experience organising small group holidays.
Flash Pack – offers boutique solo adventures for people aged 30-50.
Wild Women Expeditions – a global eco tour company offering adventure holidays for women.

Customised Organised Tours

If you like the idea of an organised holiday, but want more flexibility, some tour companies offer bespoke tailormade experiences to fit your interests and most importantly your budget.

For example, India for Beginners Tours by Breathe Dream Go, is aimed at adventuresses wanting to travel to India for the first time. They arrange bespoke tours based on your personal preferences. Breathe Dream Go is founded by Mariellen Ward, a travel writer and blogger who has travelled much of the world solo and has settled in India. If I were to choose a tour company to arrange my trip to India, I'd choose this one because I know that Mariellen lives and breathes India and, most importantly, she understands travel from the standpoint of the solo woman traveller.

The DIY Solo Traveller

If you prefer the idea of planning your own trip, and perhaps slotting in a few organised tours and experiences, I'm with you! This is my preference too - it's cheaper and offers the most flexibility. What's more, it's super easy these days to book your own flights, accommodation etc. and then plan a range of tours and experiences to suit your budget and interests. From cooking classes to safaris, city tours to guided hiking expeditions there's ample to choose from. You'll be spoilt for choice!

The benefit of this approach is that you have the complete freedom to book in some activities that really interest you, but with lots of wiggle room for a spot of sunbathing or wandering at your leisure. Furthermore, trips can often be arranged last minute, so if you're tired of beach time, you just login to your preferred excursion organiser and see what's on offer.

Useful resources for organising tours and local experiences:

Viator

Get Your Guide

Airbnb Experiences

Free Tours

Note: *always book through a reputable company, check reviews, and always avoid touts that approach you on the street offering a tour.*

It's also useful to note that free audio tours are widely available in many popular cities. These are great for self-guided free tours around museums, art galleries and tourist attractions.

Oh, and don't forget trusty guidebooks such as the *Rough Guide and Lonely Planet* – perfect for planning your own itinerary.

Retreats

Retreats are perfect for first time solo travellers. They present an opportunity to retreat from daily life and do something that you love, whilst taking care of yourself.

Perhaps when you think of the word retreat, your mind conjures up Ashrams in India or Meditation retreats in Thailand, and whilst this may tickle your fancy, retreats today come in all sorts of shapes and sizes including retreats for wellbeing, writing, cooking, art, poetry…whatever you love, there is probably a retreat out there for you.

Retreats are a way to have an immersive experience and give back to yourself. You're also likely to meet likeminded people – so there are no worries about being lonely.

Much like an organised holiday, the beauty of a retreat is that everything will be arranged for you and all you will need to do is turn up.

Volunteering

Volunteering is a great way to travel solo whilst putting back into the local community. My first experience travelling solo in Asia was through volunteering and I wholeheartedly recommend it. Volunteering gives you a very different and unique experience of the country you are visiting and allows you to gain a deeper understanding of the community you are visiting. It's also a great way to meet new people, from all walks of life.

When you volunteer, your host normally provides accommodation and food, as well as setting you up with your volunteer placement.

Choosing Your Accommodation

We all have different preferences when it comes to accommodation, and a lot will depend on your budget and your desire to interact with other people.

There's a lot of options out there – hotels, apartments, homestays, hostels, camping…

Personally, I'm a bit of a juggler, especially if I'm away for a while. I love the combination of having my own apartment within a local community, followed by a little luxury treat in a hotel and perhaps a stint in hostels for meeting fellow travellers. There's no reason why you need to stick to one type of accommodation, if you don't want to, especially as a solo traveller newbie. Try them all out and see what suits you. If the thought of staying in a hostel freaks you out, but you like the idea of budget travel, well why not just book a couple of nights in one to see how you feel? It's your trip, you have the freedom to experiment.

For example, in Penang I had a fab condominium booked out of town for a month, but I peppered the stay with trying out different hostels in the city centre. Why? Well, firstly, the hostels in Penang are gorgeous and I felt jealous of the women staying there, so I joined them! Secondly, I wanted to experience the vibrant city life at night and although my apartment was great, I didn't fancy trekking back late at night so booking a cheap hostel was just the ticket.

Whichever accommodation you decide on, make sure you keep the following in mind:

Is it in a safe location? Always check the location carefully, centre doesn't always mean city centre so check the distance carefully. You probably don't want to be out in the sticks on your first solo trip, so the location is critical. If you do decide to be further out, check transportation links.

Does it have good reviews? Whichever booking agency you use, check the reviews carefully. All online platforms have reviews and they're invaluable. Honestly, I don't give two hoots what the accommodation description says, it's the reviews that matter. Look for patterns in reviews, are lots of people saying the room was dirty? Then it probably is.

Here's a few Accommodation ideas:

Hotels & Apartments

When it comes to booking hotels many of the well-known booking agencies have loyalty programmes, therefore it makes sense to stick to one to build up those reward points and get discounts. However, it's always worth checking across sites to see if you can find a cheaper deal.

Booking.com – I tend to always use booking.com for booking hotels, because I've been using them for years and so I've built up the rewards. You can also filter the reviews by solo traveller which is very useful.

Other well-known options include Agoda, Expedia and Trip Advisor.

Houses & Apartments

Airbnb – great for booking entire houses and apartments, and rooms in shared houses. Please be mindful of checking the cancellation policy so you understand your rights; for example, when you book a place for a month any cancellation after the first 48 hours of booking is not refundable and at the hosts discretion, so you need to feel confident that you're not going to cancel.

VRBO – similar to Airbnb but has greater flexibility in relation to cancellation policies.

Hostels

Hostels have come a long way in recent years. When I first went travelling in my teens, they were somewhat rough and ready. Now approaching 50, I love hostels - there's some fabulously funky ones out there, including an increasing range of female only hostels. They're a great way to meet people and if you don't fancy sharing a dorm, many hostels have private bedrooms so you can absorb the hostel vibe whilst enjoying your privacy.

Check out:
Hostel World – probably the best booking platform for hostels. Lots of pictures and plenty of reviews.
Booking.com – not just for hotels!

Homestays

If you like the idea of staying in someone's house and getting a real feel for the local community then homestays are the way to go.

Hosts can usually give you insider knowledge about the local area, and who knows, maybe you'll make a new friend to boot.

Always book through a reputable company to ensure hosts are vetted and read the reviews.

Check out:
CouchSurfing – a well-established homestay that connects people worldwide, from the Sahara to Paris.
Workaway – if you fancy volunteering in exchange for a place to stay, Workaway is a great option. There's an awesome array of

opportunities from helping out in hostels in Mexico to picking olives in Italy.
SisterStay – is the new gal on the block and a global homestay for women over 50. Rooms have a fixed price of £36 regardless of the location and all hosts and prospective guests are verified to maintain a safe and secure environment.

Other Practical Matters

I'm not going to provide you with a list of what to pack as this information can be found easily enough elsewhere. However, here's a few essentials to think about.

Pack light

So, you want to pack 5 pairs of shoes and a wardrobe of clothes for all eventualities? Can I suggest you don't? Unless you're planning on staying in a 5-star resort and being driven from the airport to your accommodation, luggage is cumbersome, in fact if you're planning on travelling to more than one destination it's a total pain in the butt!

I'm not the greatest at packing light, and even after several years of travelling solo I still end up with unnecessary items that I just cart around. The best advice I read recently, was to lay everything out on your bed that you want to take, half it and then half it again. It's something I'm going to try my best to stick to!

If you want to know more about packing light, I recommend checking out Katherine The 5 Kilo Traveller, in Part 3, she's an expert on all things light.

Periods

If you expect Aunt Flo may show up during your time away, prepare for the fact that many countries have limited sanitary options, especially tampons, so if you use tampons pack enough to last the duration of your time away.

As an alternative, consider a reusable menstrual cup. I swapped over to a cup several years ago whilst travelling and have used it ever since. Menstrual cups are an eco-alternative to disposable sanitary protection. They are considerably better for the environment and a big money saver.

Phone plan

If you don't want to be hit by extortionate charges, check your phone plan before you leave. If your plan doesn't include roaming to your specific destination, you can either check to see if you can upgrade your plan – many mobile phone providers have an option for adding on an international package or alternatively, buy a local sim when you arrive at your destination.

Bank Card

If there's one thing you'll need when you travel, it's money and whilst you may feel your regular bank card is your best option, I'd advise you to get an international bank card. When you pay with your regular bank card, you're hit with high ATM fees (2-4% on each transaction) and whilst it may not seem like a lot, it adds up. Also, with increased bank security, you may find your card is declined when you use it abroad as it will be noted as unusual activity, unless of course you notify your bank first.

An easier option is to get one of the new generation travel debit cards. Honestly, banking internationally has never been so easy.

The benefits include:

- The ability to load multiple currencies so that you can pay with the local currency wherever you are.
- Reduced ATM fees
- Solid app security

Chapter 13

USEFUL APPS

Apps have made travel significantly easier and safer. Here's a few of many to peruse:

Practical Apps

Maps.me – for downloadable offline maps, perfect for when you don't have Wi-Fi.

Google Translate – it's likely you'll need some translation help at some point, so having the Google Translate app is ideal. You can type, text, speak and take a photo of the text you want translated.

XE Currency Converter – provides free mid-market exchange rates.

Kayak, Momondo, Google Flights, Skyscanner – choose your favourite app for booking flights. I check them all for the best flight deals.

Rideshare apps – it's always useful to have the local rideshare app so that you can book a car with ease. The main ones are:

Uber – operates in 65 countries

Lyft – US and Canada

Grab – Southeast Asia

Trail Wallet – a travel budget app for tracking expenses.

Mayday Safety – a personal safety app, which alerts family and friends with your exact location.

TripScout – features the best articles and videos from top publishers and local influencers for each destination. Select a location of interest, customise your feed and wambam you'll be sent interesting and pertinent articles based on your personal preferences. Great for pre-trip planning.

TripIt – places all your travel information in one place, so as soon as you book a flight, hotel, or car reservations you forward it to the app and everything is stored for that trip.

FlightAware – live tracking of flights, perfect for those nervous prone individuals waiting at home for a flight to arrive.

Meeting People and Connecting with People

Tourlina – a women only app that helps you to connect with both local and travelling women in 160 countries.

Meetup – helps you discover things to do with other people in the local area.

Facebook – join Facebook groups for women travellers. These are great for asking questions, getting support from like-minded women and even finding a buddy to meet up with in a location.

There are many to choose from, including: Solo Female Traveller Network, Wanderful, Girls Love Travel, Women Who Travel, Girls Gone Global, Over 40 – The Solo Female Traveller Network.

Chapter 14

PRACTISING PRESENCE

Always say 'yes' to the present moment…
Surrender to what is.
Say 'yes' to life
and see how life starts suddenly to start working for you rather than against you.

– Eckhart Tolle

We have talked about the value of being more mindful or present throughout this book.

Mindfulness can be of great benefit to the mind and body as a tool for maintaining healthy relationships.

The idea behind mindfulness is straightforward enough, it simply means paying attention to your thoughts without judging them. Through regular practice, being mindful enables you to bring a greater awareness to thoughts that are unhelpful and although it is impossible to get rid of negative thoughts completely, we can get better at consciously picking thoughts that are healthy and be more aware of those that aren't, like picking apples from a tree.

Mindfulness is tricky, especially at first, but with practice, it becomes easier. The most important thing is to just go with the flow and enjoy it. Don't chastise yourself if your thoughts wander, they are bound to – that's what our brains do. Just bring yourself back to the present moment and acknowledge your wandering thoughts. It's in that moment of catching your wandering thoughts, that you have increased your level of consciousness and that's mindfulness.

There are many great books and apps dedicated to teaching mindfulness. I'd recommend finding a resource that works for you. There will be some techniques that resonate and others that don't. If at first you don't connect with a method, try something else.

I'll be honest, I don't have one specific 'mindful meditation.' I have several little strategies, for example I like to imagine placing my unhealthy and habitual thoughts into a little bubble so they can float away and pop…so they do not impinge on my daily happiness. I also began practicing yoga regularly several years ago, and through the awareness of the breath and practising breathing techniques, meditation and mindfulness are a happy side effect.

Here's a few tips for focusing on the present moment

Focus on your breathing - focus on your breath as it moves in and out of your body. As thoughts arise, do not judge them, just observe them. Pay particular attention to the out breath and the feeling of space that follows, just before you breathe in again.

Pay attention - take the time to really experience your environment with all your senses – touch, sound, sight, smell and taste. For example, when you eat, eat slowly, savour the flavours and smells.

Body awareness meditation - lie down, focus your attention slowly and deliberately on each part of your body, from your toes to your head. Be aware of any sensations, emotions or thoughts that come up as you move up your body. Don't judge the thoughts, just observe them. If any negative thoughts surface, you could allow them to flow out through your toes.

Walking meditation - find a suitable place to walk, I'd suggest somewhere peaceful. Take a few minutes to ground yourself and pay full attention to your body. Sense how the ground feels beneath your feet. As you slowly walk, be aware of the different sensations in your body, and your thoughts and feelings. Again, don't judge those thoughts and feelings, just consciously observe them.

For more guidance, see Appendix 1: Resources.

Appendix 1: RESOURCES

Book Recommendations

Relationships

Loving Bravely 20 Lessons of Self-Discovery to help you Get the Love you Want by Alexandra H. Solomon
Mindful Relationships by Oli Doyle

Solo Travel

Alone Time by Stephanie Rosenbloom
Tales of a Female Nomad: Living at Large in the World by Rita Golden Gelman

Practicing Presence/Mindfulness

A New Earth by Eckhart Tolle
Mindful Relationships by Oli Doyle

Websites

Relationships & Self Development
Psychologies: *www.psychologies.co.uk*
Psychology Today: *www.psychologytoday.com*
Relate the Relationship People:
www.relate.org.uk/relationship-advice

Mindfulness

Headspace: *www.headspace.com*
Mindful: *www.mindful.org*

Podcasts

Personal Growth Through Adventure
Into the Woods: *www.hollyworton.com/podcast*

REFERENCES

Augsburger, D W. (1982). *Caring Enough to Hear and Be Heard.* VA: Herald Press

Coelho, P. (1992). *The Pilgrimage*. UK: HarperCollins Publishers

Cain, S. (2012). *The Power of Introverts in a World That Can't Stop Talking*

Campbell, J. (1991). *The Power of Myth*. New York: Anchor Books

Doyle, O. (2019). *Mindful Relationships: Build nurturing, meaningful relationships by living in the present moment.* London: The Orion Publishing Company Ltd

Gilbert, E. (2007). *Eat, Pray, Love: One Woman's Search for Everything Across Italy, India and Indonesia*. New York: Riverhead Books

Lesser, E. (2004). *Broken Open: How difficult times can help us grow.* New York: Vintage Publishing

Rosenbloom, S. (2019). *Alone Time: Four Cities, four seasons and the pleasure of solitude.* London: Transworld Publishing

Solomon, A. (2019). *Loving Bravely: 20 Lessons of Self-Discovery to Help You Get the Love You Want.* US: New Harbinger Publications

Thomashauer, R. (2004). *Mama Gena's Marriage Manual.* New York: Simon and Schuster

Tolle, E. (2004). *The Power of Now: A Guide to Spiritual Enlightenment.* California: New World Library

Websites

Alexander, E. (2019). 5 Reasons solo travel is good is good for your relationship. Harpers Bazaar. 5 reasons solo travel is good for your relationship (*harpersbazaar.com*)

Bonier, A. (2018). 7 Ways to Build Trust in a Relationship. Psychology Today. *www.psychologytoday.com/us/blog/friendship-20/201812/7-ways-build-trust-in-relationship*

Carter, S B. (2012). 6 Reasons You Should Spend More Time Alone. Psychology Today. *www.psychologytoday.com/us/blog/high-octane-women/201201/6-reasons-you-should-spend-more-time-alone*

Martin, JG. (2018). Why more and more people are choosing to travel solo. Lonely Planet. Why solo travel is on the rise in countries around the world (*lonelyplanet.com*)

Mutanda, A. (2015). Four steps to setting healthy boundaries in your relationship. Relate: the relationship people. *www.relate.org.uk/blog/2015/2/17/four-steps-setting-healthy-boundaries-your-relationship*

Ng, A. (2022). Why solo female travelers are joining group tours. CNBC. *www.cnbc.com/2022/05/03/female-solo-travel-should-i-join-a-group-tour-alone.html*

Solo Traveller (2022). Solo Travel Statistics and Data 2021 – 2022. Solo Travel Statistics and Data: 2021 -2022 - Solo Traveler (*solotravelerworld.com*)

Weiser, K. (2021). How Journaling can improve your wellbeing. Psychologies. How journaling can improve your well-being | Psychologies

ABOUT THE AUTHOR

Jenny Mowbray is a passionate solo travel writer, who aims to inspire those on the cusp of realising their own wanderlust. When she is not travelling solo, Jenny divides her time between the UK and Italy where she and her partner are slowly renovating a house in a picturesque hilltop town. She's an enthusiastic advocate of living a freedom orientated lifestyle, one rich in experience and growth. She loves cooking, travelling, hiking and yoga. Jenny writes about her experiences and shares her verve for the world on her website Orchids to Olives.

You can find Jenny at:

www.orchids-to-olives.com

Instagram: www.instagram.com/orchids_to_olives

Facebook: www.facebook.com/Orchids-to-Olives

A Request

If you enjoyed this book, I'd love you to write a quick review online. It only takes a couple of minutes, yet it can make a big difference. Good reviews help other readers to find new books, and who knows your review could inspire someone else to follow their dreams. It would also make my day – I'd love to hear from you!

Thank you so much,

Jenny

Printed in Great Britain
by Amazon